When Caring Hurts

For families in chaos

Alisa Carraro

This book is not intended as medical, psychological, or legal advice. It is for educational purposes only. Readers should consult qualified professionals for personalized guidance.

ISBN: 978-1-0677909-0-5
Cover Design: Carraro Media
Interior Design: Carraro Media
Printed by Ingram Spark's global print network.
Proudly written and published in Canada.

First Edition: August, 2026

Dedication

This book is dedicated to my mom, Resy (Teresa). I love you with all my heart. My heart will always miss you and carry the ache of a memory that never fades. I feel it too, the longing you carried for family when time distanced them or carried them away. Thank you for your longevity, your quiet determination, and your lifelong loyalty to us. Please know that I understood. And I will never, ever forget.

TABLE OF CONTENTS

Appendix

About The Author

PREFACE

The Realities of Caregiving

A truth reveals itself the moment you step into caregiving: the transition is unforeseeable, and it reshapes you before you even realize it's happening. Caregiving changes you. It is inevitable. It reshapes your lifestyle, your identity, your balance and your sense of what's possible. It asks more of you than what is obvious. It stretches you in ways you never expected. And it often leaves you feeling like you're steering a path in a world no one prepared you for. A world that restricts you, at times, cages you. A world that changes on a dime. Sometimes positively, sometimes negatively.

My desire to write this book was because even though I had adapted to this transition, nothing prepared me for what was about to happen to my role as caregiver when my mother developed dementia. Suddenly, all my freedoms were restrained. I didn't have any. It was as if someone took me from my community and, I didn't even know when. What was supposed to be a few days stay, turned out to be years. I began meeting people who were living inside the same restrictive and chaotic world. People much like me who were overwhelmed, exhausted, and doing their best in circumstances that would break most. Clients who loved deeply but were drowning quietly. People who blamed themselves for circumstances that were never their fault; who thought they were failing when they were actually carrying the weight of everything on their shoulders.

This book is about compassion and giving language to the invisible. It's about helping families reunite and live again. And mostly, it is about making sense of what happens to you when you are the one that has to facilitate caring, when no one else is willing to step up. You know you can't walk away because it isn't in your nature to abandon family. It is about showing those who are silent in their role, I see you. And together, we can get through this to emerge stronger, understood, seen and loved.

INTRODUCTION

Caring for someone you love can be one of the most gratifying experiences of a lifetime. It can draw you into a journey that feels meaningful, intimate, and profound. Yet, it can also become one of the most overwhelming chapters of life you will ever face. Especially true when the timing of care doesn't align with your perceived future. Especially so, when it is thrusted upon you without permission. All of a sudden, you are the caregiver. You are the one that will have to be there, to manage a home no one else wants to manage.

When unexpected circumstances like an illness appear in your reality, you are left gripping for fixes with no clear outcomes in place. When dementia enters the home, or when PTSD defines the rhythm of your day, things change rapidly. Unless you have experience with this kind of life change, anxiety often follows closely behind. The home atmosphere undergoes an erratic shift. The shift is often unpleasant and very present. You find yourself wondering when trauma suddenly slipped through the front door, uninvited to bring chaos in. You find yourself out of your element and out of your authority. What once felt predictable, effortless love suddenly becomes heavy, disoriented and unbearably hard to hold.

Most families don't realize any of this is happening at first. They think they're dealing with temporary behaviours that are fixable problems or simply "difficult days." They trust time will shift back to normalcy; a this too shall pass belief. But underneath it all; underneath confusion, fear, exhaustion; there is a whole other reality forming. The home life is now affected by a buildup of nervous tension. All the while you to try your best to survive, deeply buried under responsibility.

Did you know that when one person's neurology is overwhelmed, the entire family feels it too?

There is always more than not, one major player who holds everything together in a family dynamic. And usually, these caring individuals love deeply but are stretched thin. Many adult children are trying to support a parent with dementia while managing their own life, their own stresses and often their own careers. They are the sandwiched generation who watch time fast forward; the caregiver asking themselves when did so many years flash by and they think to themselves but "I haven't done that thing." They observe loved ones walk on eggshells around trauma responses. They are families who feel they're living in chaos and can't figure out why nothing seems to help.

This could be you. You might be that over-tired caregiver, or maybe the confused one; the one doing everything you can and still wondering why it feels like you're falling short. You keep going but the circle you're running keeps widening, and you quietly ask yourself, "When did all the straight lines disappear?"

Caring for a loved one is a lot. It's emotionally charged, psychologically demanding, and often far more cumbrous than anyone on the outside can see. When the illness is chronic rather than short-term, the weight doesn't lift and you carry it continuously, without real breaks or time to reset. Caregivers of dementia understand this.

When the load becomes that laborious, it makes sense that you start to feel different. You're still functional, but not quite yourself. Your body shifts into a mode that helps you keep going without pause. It goes into an autopilot state; a natural response to prolonged stress. A quiet signal that exposes just how much you've been holding together for so long.

You try really hard, yet some days it still feels like you're falling behind. It might very well be that your nerves are just overwhelmed. And most likely, your family's nerves too. This is when chaos begins.

The best gift you can give yourself now, is to pause and begin understanding the chaos.

In the chapters ahead, you'll get insight into how trauma, dementia, chronic stress, and anxiety affect the brain and body. You'll learn why communication breaks down, why emotions escalate, why shutdown happens, and why caring feels like chaos even when you're doing everything "right." You'll learn what a nervous system breakdown actually is; and how to get through it with clarity and compassion.

Most importantly, you'll learn how to support the people you love without losing yourself in the process, especially your mind. Even when it feels unbearable and gloomy because it can get better for you. Hope is woven into every small act of care you give.

In my own journey of caring, I found I needed help but the help I required wasn't textbook. And there weren't agencies out there that fit my mother's needs or our personal unique family need. She wasn't ever ill enough, or dependant enough for them to provide her with the care she ought to receive; caring for her was a full-time job. I found myself so alone even when community resources said the "right" thing, I knew the moment the phone call ended, or the worker would exit the door, we were on our own again. It was hurtful. It left me feeling abandoned and alone. Everything was on my shoulders. And it was becoming too much. I was always exhausted. Not just physically but it had become an emotional and mental exhaustion as well. This went on for a prolonged period of time. The turning point came when I began researching and boy, did I research. I was already a coach by profession. I decided to take the same approach to our family situation and enrolled in courses, seminars, classes, subscriptions etc. The alone feeling began to fade as I listened to stories and others working through the same issues. I learned that many were in the same boat. I saw other individuals struggle. And I realized from observation and statistics; getting outside help for my mother was still going to be a very long struggle.

I tried "talking" to support workers, but everything stayed in a loop. The advice was textbook, or at times it felt like a professional courtesy, a script and I didn't feel I was making any strides because things would just rebound back to how they were before. Until one day, it dawned on me that I needed in the moment support. My friends couldn't fully understand my situation because they hadn't lived it, and I felt like I would be burdening them if I reached out. It didn't feel right anymore. What was going to shift this state?

I understood what I needed and soon realized what I wanted was something actionable and immediate. Booking an appointment for next week or a month from now was not going to satisfy the crisis moment. It was in a moment of sheer crisis and isolation, that I began creating apps to lighten the load of caregiving and crisis. I found myself in front of my laptop researching the process of coding and data. Months of building helped me see how hopeful the situation actually was. I needed something I could utilize when we were in crisis. The apps became my go-to resource, helping me remember what to say and why my mother behaved the way she did. When you're overwhelmed, the brain simply forgets. These apps (which you can find at the end of my book) were my saviour. And in the chapters ahead, I want you to feel that same relief. This book is, in many ways, the manual behind the calmative and cumulative resources that carried me through what I call the darkest of days.

My hope is this book can be for many a companion, something you can open on the hardest day or night, and feel less alone. When at 3am, you can't get back to sleep and no one wants to hear how much in a panic you are. This book can be something that helps you understand what's happening beneath the insomnia. Something that gives you workable tools for your homefront and family when under stress.

And remember that in caregiving, you don't need perfection or superhuman strength; though it is often demanded of you. What you want to maintain is your nurture, your compassion, the reason you began your journey in the first place; because the core within every caregiver - is love.

As I write this book, it is my hope to offer understanding, support and a balanced voice in the middle of the chaos.

Take a breath.
Settle in.
You don't have to hold all of this alone anymore. We can journey this part together. So, here goes

PART I

FOR FAMILIES IN CHAOS

Knock, knock. Look who dropped in: Dementia and PTSD. How lovely - they just invited themselves in. They're already redesigning the house, everyone's sleep patterns, and every reaction in between. And look, they brought a friend: anxiety, the background noise of daily life. Come on in, join the trauma that now echoes through the walls and even sits down at family dinners. Does any of this sound familiar?

Unexpected patterns like these can manifest into the family silently, when you least expect it like intruders or they can manifest as friction, loud behaviour and tension. Either way the patterns emerge, they force families to operate in survival mode as they begin to tear at the fabric. People stop responding from their values and start responding from nervous reactions. Conversations become shorter. Patience wears thin. Small triggers turn into big emotions. Everyone feels like they're walking through the same storm but experiencing different weather.

Most families blame themselves for this. They think they should be coping better. They think other families would handle it differently. In fact, they are sure other families would handle it better. So, no one talks about it to avoid the shame or embarrassment.

This section will help you understand what's really goes on when this happens. You'll learn how all this stress affects the nervous system and why it crashes under chronic exposure; why trauma responses spread to everyone close by, and why caregiving especially in dementia, PTSD, and anxiety creates patterns that feel impossible to escape.

You'll also learn something most families never hear: everything you are experiencing is normal. Other families feel it too. Your reactions, exhaustion, confusion is all normal.

It is part of the overwhelm, and now your nervous system needs to be addressed.

Clarity will help you finally find a way to interrupt the chaos head on, by giving you a way to heal your nerves – something that may be a long time overdue.

SECTION I - Understanding the Chaos

CHAPTER 1

WHEN THE FAMILY NUCLEUS BREAKS

What is breaking? Most people imagine it as something shattering- a collapse, a crisis, a moment where everything falls apart at once. Boom. You explode, the world ends, and the dark that once lived as a shadow suddenly becomes a vast, endless void. It feels final.

But in reality, the neurology behind your nerves doesn't usually snap in a single moment. Nerves adapt to their environment within the human body while often becoming resilient to stressors. Until the moment the body weakens from the silent, unresolved overload.

Nerves are part of an intricate nervous system that send signals throughout the entire body. Composed of two parts: central and peripheral which includes the brain, spinal cord and nerves all working together. Neurons are fundamental units that communicate through electrochemical signals coordinating cognitive and physiological responses within the nervous system. Neurons integrate enormous amounts of information and also activate responses to both internal and external stimulation. Environments matter. Both internal and external. This means each family member and the home environment matter in order to co-exist happily.

When the nervous system begins to break down, it expresses itself outwardly from the body in altering behaviour. As you care for a loved one, the weight of responsibility and chronic uncertainty accumulate to create a tipping point, further exasperated by unrest and trauma. While this is happening to one member, it slowly starts to happen to the rest of the family as well.

I remember a kinesiologist telling me years ago that when you start releasing old patterns, the people closest to you often begin releasing theirs too. So, it makes sense that the opposite is also true: when you're in crisis, tense, or agitated, your loved ones will feel it - and often become it.

As a result, the family nucleus starts to fray. Each person can no longer stay calm within unpredictability. And you can no longer be a caregiver holding everyone together while inside, you are falling apart. Your own fragility and needs are buried beneath the invisible shield that once kept the household together but now, brings everything down.

All of a sudden, you become short tempered. And so do other members. You've been strong for too long and adapted to a role without support. Your reaction times shorten. Your patience and stability crack. You basically short circuit your internal wiring; your neurons misfire because you are overloaded. Your nerves once responded in a predictable organized pattern, fire hazardless, shooting every imaginable way. And your external environment reacts to it.

The slow erosion of capacity

It is important to understand every nervous system has limits; as does every caregiver as well as every loved one.

When you're caring for someone with dementia, or living with a loved one who has PTSD, or raising children where trauma exists, these limits are tested daily. You're not just managing tasks, you're managing emotions, behaviors, triggers, confusion, fear, and the invisible tension that fills the space between each individual.

At first, you cope. You learn to adapt. You push through and learn to push harder. This is the pattern. And you don't mind. Your incredible discipline earns you structure and stability, at first, it pays off.

Eventually, without realizing it, you cross the threshold where your nerves can no longer regulate like before because you become overwhelmed with stress.

This is the moment families describe as:

- "I don't recognize myself anymore."
- "I'm always on edge."
- "I can't think straight."
- "I'm exhausted but can't rest."
- "I'm either numb or overwhelmed."
- "Everything feels like too much."
- "I feel like I am running circles."

And now, the looping circle with all its repetition...just got wider.

The body's emergency mode

When the nervous system becomes overwhelmed, it shifts into survival mode as it is instinctively programmed to do. This is hard wired in our core. The body learns to prioritize safety over connection, protection over presence, reaction over reflection.

You may notice:

- A shorter fuse
- Difficulty concentrating
- Feeling constantly "on alert"

- Emotional numbness
- Mental numbness
- Trouble sleeping
- Feeling detached or disconnected
- Overreacting to small things
- Feeling like you're "shutting down"

These are survival responses pure and simple. They are programmed and automatic.

Your body is trying to protect you from what it perceives as ongoing threat; whether that threat is dementia-related behaviors, unpredictable trauma responses, or the relentless pressure of caregiving. This is the hardest point of realization. Seeing yourself here. Alone, burnt out and misunderstood.

Why caregiving accelerates breakdown

Caregiving, especially in the context of dementia, PTSD, and anxiety creates a unique kind of stress. It's not a single event. It's not a crisis that ends. It's a constant, unpredictable, emotionally loaded environment that keeps your nervous system activated for extremely long periods of time.

This is why caregivers often say:

- "I never get a break."
- "I'm always waiting for the next thing to happen."
- "I can't relax, even when things are calm."

Your neurological system is doing exactly what it was designed to do: scan for danger, anticipate needs, and stay alert. But when this becomes your daily reality, your system never gets to reset.

Over time, this can lead to:

- Hypervigilance
- Emotional exhaustion
- Cognitive fatigue
- Irritability
- Shutdown
- Burnout
- Mental exhaustion

This is the loop that gets every caregiver. It ebbs away at your self confidence that has slowly declined. But you keep at it: doing too much, for too long, without any lasting support.

The moment you realize something has shifted

You won't notice the breakdown while it's happening. You'll notice it when you hit rock bottom or a moment where you can't push through anymore.

For some, the nervous shift reveals itself as a sudden emotional collapse. For others, it can be a quiet numbness. But for many, it's a sense of losing themselves and the beginning of complete detachment.

You may find yourself thinking:

- "I don't know how much more I can take."
- "I feel like I'm disappearing."
- "I'm not myself anymore."
- "I'm scared of my own reactions."
- "I feel invisible."

These are the signs of complete overwhelm! Your brain has become an over loaded circuit board with too many neurons firing at once. Or not at all, when the circuit burns out.

Overwhelm is a real, tangible state - not imagined. You're not suddenly "out of control" or acting out in ways people label as bad behaviour. You don't develop these reactions because you're unstable or "psycho." People say that, I know. When you fray, you become "that psycho." When you raise your voice to be heard, suddenly you're aggressive. It's uncomfortable, and it's unfair. Add cultural behaviours and reactions to the mix, and communication becomes a minefield. One thing is certain: this is the moment you need to unplug for a while.

Some cultures naturally express emotion with more volume or intensity, especially when passion rises. This isn't anger; it's simply another form of heartfelt communication. It's important to recognize that not everyone interprets these expressions the same way, and people who come from quieter or more reserved communication styles may understandably feel affected by it.

At the same time, no one should be expected to change the core of who they are to make their way of expressing emotion more palatable to others. Healthy relationships, especially within culturally diverse families, require space for different communication styles to coexist. This is where language, understanding, and tolerance become essential.

When diversity enters a family, experiences of communication, comprehension, and emotional expression will not always align. These differences can come from culture, generation, or personal history. Staying united requires a willingness on all sides to understand each other beyond labels or clinical interpretations.

This is not about excusing boundary crossing; boundaries matter for everyone involved. It's about recognizing that fundamentals can remain intact while still making room for each person's authentic expression. Ultimately, the goal is a return to love - because love, more than anything else, is the universal language that bridges these differences.

Why understanding matters

It is really important to become aware of your surroundings. You can't change what you don't understand or heal what you blame yourself for. How can you regulate what you believe might be a personal weakness without realizing what is at the root of it and the behaviour that has sprung from it? Especially now that we understand what over-burden and stress place on the intricate neurological responses of the nervous system - and how deeply connected and correlated those signals are to your functioning as a whole.

Understanding nervous system breakdowns gives you:

- Communication (language) for what you are experiencing
- Compassion for yourself
- Clarity about what's happening in your home
- A roadmap for change
- **Permission to stop carrying the shame**

This chapter is the chance to initiate and finally begin the process of unleashing the shackles and burden of the on-going chaos. The beginning of the release; the moment you can stop and actually feel your heart beating again.

In the chapters to follow, you'll have the chance to learn what happens inside the brain and body during chronic stress; how trauma responses spread through families; and why caregiving environments become chaotic even when everyone is trying their best.

But most of all, you will learn that families can heal. The break in unity is not permanent though it feels like it is. Fibers can reknit. Your family though stretched, weakened, conflicted and distant can stabilize and become a team again.

And always remember, you have come this far! And that is a lot to be proud of.

CHAPTER 2

TRAUMA ACTIVE FAMILIES

This chapter was extremely sensitive for me to write for many reasons. I come from trauma. I had been exposed to it many years before my mother developed dementia. I have also helped many of my clients overcome their own traumatic experiences whether it be in relationships or at work, or within their family dynamics as well. You would be surprised how many people feel alone in their trauma. Even with all the social media, all the tools out there, all the exposure and activity, people still feel the reality that caring hurts. Most families don't realize they are trauma active. They think they are merely stressed. It is a combination of not knowing and denial. Often chalked up to being tired, not communicating well, dealing with personality differences, bad days, or emotional sensitivity. Maybe, the fine line is hard to distinguish but often these can be signs of trauma:

- irritability
- withdrawal
- shutting down
- overexplaining/overreacting
- walking on eggshells
- avoiding conflict
- trying to keep the peace
- feeling responsible for everyone's emotions
- insomnia

As someone who has experienced chronic trauma, I have learned that trauma shows up in the nervous system long before it shows up as a behaviour. We are physically affected, and we don't realize it.

Sometimes, we do realize it and think we are taking the right steps to heal. But often, we fail to recognize the triggers because we are still being traumatized in one way or another, And, when one person in a family carries trauma, the entire family feels the ripple effect. How many of us experienced this as children? When we were little, we were affected. If mom, dad, or a sibling, heck our teacher was upset, we often became sad or worried. We would cry or pout, or even panic. These experiences are very real and internalized without realizing it. But this is also the evolution of the life. Trauma is everywhere. It is woven through more of our world than we care to admit.

What It Means to Live with Trauma

When one family member starts the journey of self-awareness, it doesn't always sit well with the rest of the family. Self-awareness requires change and a hard look at the facts: what is really in front of you, not the version of reality you have tricked yourself to believe is in front of you. The subconscious or ego is often afraid of failure, or loss etc., that is why it doesn't admit to the facts. It knows how to protect you and your family. It does the job very well. The key message I want readers to hear is that a trauma active family is not a "broken" family. It is literally a family that is active in trauma.

It's a family that has lived through more than most people will ever understand and the experience is unique to the family. Once healed, the trauma can be the beacon, the light that shapes the path and creates an ever-lasting journey that does not crumble the structure but rather fortifies it, like the great architectures of human history still standing today! But this journey, is life long. And once you start it, it is impossible to turn your back on it.

Let's look at what trauma may be:

- a veteran returning home with invisible wounds or physical wounds
- a parent who grew up in chaos or abuse or abandonment
- a child who experienced medical trauma or chronic illness
- a partner living with anxiety or panic
- children of divorce, or losing a family member when young
- a caregiver supporting someone with dementia or mental illness
- a family member who survived violence, loss, or instability
- school children being ridiculed or who experience severe judgement and punishment.
- war and disease
- experiencing bullying, shaming or ridicule
- etc.

In simple terms, trauma is anything that overwhelms you and leaves a lasting imprint.

When trauma centers, it doesn't stay contained. It spreads through patterns, reactions, expectations, and emotions. We all experienced Covid-19, remember the effect it had on the entire planet? Trauma spreading is a version of COVID. It can be seen, unseen, silent but effective. And it can shape not only the community but the planet.

How Trauma Shapes Daily Life

Unfortunately, trauma changes human behaviour in many ways. It has been observed to change the way people:

- communicate
- interpret tone
- respond to stress
- handle conflict
- trust others
- regulate emotions

- connect in relationships

In environments where trauma is active you may notice:

1. Hypervigilance

Someone is always scanning for danger, even when nothing is wrong.

2. Emotional Over-reactions

Small triggers lead to big responses because the nervous system is already overloaded.

3. Shutdown or Numbing

When emotions feel too big, the body protects itself by going quiet. Even freezing.

4. Avoidance

Conversations, tasks, or memories that feel overwhelming get pushed aside.

5. Walking on Eggshells

Family members adjust their behaviour to prevent conflict or emotional explosions.

6. Misunderstandings

Trauma filters how people hear each other, often turning neutral comments into perceived threats.

7. Cycles of Conflict and Repair

Arguments repeat because the underlying nervous patterns haven't changed.

Key components to remember:

None of this is intentional, personal and definitely not a sign of failure.

It's a natural built in bodily response that actually reshapes the family environment.

Why Trauma Responses Spread

Humans regulate through each other: we co-regulate and co-dysregulate.

Women see this first-hand. When women live together, it's common to notice the cycles shifting and seeming to align. I experienced this in university - a house full of women, and somehow, we all ended up getting our monthly visit within days of each other. Whether it was biology, bonding, or simply shared rhythms, our bodies responded to one another. And if our bodies can attune like that, it makes perfect sense that stress and chaos can ripple through a household too. We evolve in patterns shaped by chemistry, connection, and environment - and our bodily chemistry is always in motion.

So, when one person's nerves are overwhelmed, others feel it. This is something we forget in the moment. When one person shuts down, others compensate. When one person is anxious, those closest absorb the tension and adapt.

The Invisible Load of Trauma in Caregiving

Caregivers carry a unique burden:

- They manage their own stress
- They manage the emotional climate
- They anticipate triggers
- They soften their tone
- They adjust their expectations
- They absorb the reactions of others
- They hold the family together
- And often, manifest subclinical environmental stress responses

This is why caregivers often say:

- "I feel like I'm the only adult here."
- "I'm always the one calming everyone down."
- "I can't ever relax."
- "I'm tired of being the strong one."

This is not imagined. This very real and very common. It is a caregiver feeling the trauma from the chaos. And carrying more than they can cope with; but somehow still doing it.

The Difference Between Trauma, Stress, and Burnout

Many families confuse these three states, but they're not the same.

Stress

A temporary response to pressure.
You can recover with rest.

Burnout

A prolonged state of exhaustion.
You feel depleted, detached, and overwhelmed.

Trauma

A nervous system injury.
It changes how you respond to the world.

Families often live with all three at once.

Why This Chapter Matters

This chapter is important in naming or identifying what is really going on in your own family or individual life. As much as this is for families, it can also speak to an individual. The research and resources are the same.

A key step towards growth and creating change is identifying the situation in order to heal. This is when the awareness peaks to a defined point. And here, you can make a conscious choice. By pin pointing a pattern or patterns, you then realize you can break them. This helps you detach from taking things personally. Once you understand the dynamic response because of triggers, it is no longer personalized. You will start to support the family and yourself beyond personal attacks because you won't feel them the same.

This part is huge; a transformational milestone in balancing sensitivities. This is where you begin creating a life that functions, one where you are at the wheel. A life where you choose your reactions, your responses, and the moments you engage, attend, do, smile, breathe. It gives you permissions you may never have allowed yourself before. And it enhances your life in far more areas than you expect, because the effect reaches outward.

You will notice how immediate being in the moment of your truth feels. It brings a sense of wholeness, unity, and freedom. There will be days when it still feels foreign or uncomfortable. There may be days when you buckle. But every step is victorious, because you will know you are at the wheel.

This chapter hopefully gave you language for what you've been living through and helped you identify the patterns. It also showed why listening to your nerves - your state of being - is more important than the behaviour. When you recognize the trauma, the "problem" stops being the focus; regulating your nerves becomes the path forward.

And most importantly: in the next chapter, we'll explore how dementia, PTSD, and anxiety create the perfect storm inside a home, and why caregiving becomes so emotionally complex. This is the chaos.

CHAPTER 3

DEMENTIA, PTSD, ANXIETY: THE PERFECT STORM

Some families live with stress, manage it and move on. Families in chaos often live with several forms of stress, often at the same time.

It is understood that dementia changes the brain. PTSD creates neurological changes. Anxiety changes the body's sense of safety. What a combination when all three are actively engaging in the family's dynamic.

When these conditions exist under the same roof or even within the same person, the emotional climate or the individual becomes unpredictable, overwhelmed, and exhausting. The brain and body are simply trying to survive experiences they were not designed to handle alone; whether being it or being in it.

This chapter explores how these conditions collide, amplify each other, and create the "perfect storm" that so many families endure.

Dementia: The Unpredictable Disruptor

When my mother experienced dementia, it did not clinically appear in her brain scans. My mother was not diagnosed with Alzheimer's. Her doctor stated her brain scans were "unremarkable." But yet, dementia began. Once it took it's first step, the decline was gradual but permanent. The steps downward began to appear. The doctor helped me understand that dementia progresses in steps, much like a stairway. It drops, then plateaus for a while, then drops further then plateaus again and so forth. This is contrary to Alzheimer's where the slope is a sharp, steady decline like a steep hill. I found some relief in this as I understood there could be time to adjust and cope with the changes in my mom's behaviours and moods in the months ahead. This gave me a flicker of hope. Though sudden to us, this gave me time to research and learn everything I could about it and caregiving. I was not ready for any of it.

The more I researched; I learned dementia doesn't just affect memory. It affects:

- emotional regulation
- impulse control
- communication
- perception
- the ability to understand context
- the ability to filter sensory input

This means a person with dementia may:

- misinterpret your tone
- feel threatened by routine changes
- become overwhelmed by noise or movement
- react strongly to confusion
- lash out when scared
- withdraw when overstimulated

These reactions are not intentional. At first, you yourself may feel as if everything is personal. Until you realise, your loved one's behaviours are neurologically based.

To the family, they often always feel personal.

A caregiver may think:

- “Why are they angry at me?”
- “Why won’t they listen?”
- “Why does everything turn into a fight?”

The answer is simple yet painful:

Their brain is losing the ability to interpret the world as it once knew; safely.

And when someone’s brain can’t create safety, family or the caregiver take over the job, often at a cost.

PTSD: The Invisible Alarm System

PTSD is not a memory problem. Though a symptom of it can be loss of memory, especially short-term. It is however, a threat-detection problem.

The entire neurological body becomes stuck in survival mode, constantly scanning for danger, even when none exists. This is also an anxiety response. The two are often twins. Those who have PTSD also express anxiety. This creates:

- hypervigilance
- irritability
- intense emotional reactivity
- avoidance
- nightmares
- shutdown
- difficulty concentrating
- exaggerated startle responses
- elevated levels of cortisol
- musculoskeletal pain and inflammation

In a family, PTSD often looks like:

- walking on eggshells
- unpredictable emotional spikes
- sudden withdrawal
- tension that fills the room
- arguments that escalate quickly
- a member who seems "far away"
- a parent or member who can't tolerate noise or chaos

PTSD doesn't just solely affect the person who carries it; it affects everyone who loves them.

Anxiety: The Constant Background Noise

Anxiety is often dismissed as "worry," but physiologically, it is a state of chronic activation. The body is flooded with signals that say:

- "Something is wrong."
- "Something bad is coming."
- "You're not safe."

Even when nothing is happening.

Anxiety creates:

- restlessness
- irritability
- difficulty sleeping, insomnia
- muscle tension
- racing thoughts
- emotional overwhelm
- difficulty making decisions, indecisiveness

In a family, anxiety spreads quickly. One person's fear becomes

everyone's tension.
One persons' overwhelm becomes the household's atmosphere. And from there a whole other subgroup of illnesses or issues can arise. As an example: anorexia, insomnia, IBS or digestive related issues, OCD or addictive behavior etc.

The Collision

Now imagine a home where:

- dementia causes confusion and emotional outbursts
- PTSD creates hypervigilance and reactivity
- anxiety amplifies every stressor
- caregiving responsibilities never end
- trauma history shapes communication
- sleep is disrupted
- routines are unpredictable
- everyone is exhausted

This isn't a "difficult home." But to an outsider, it sure looks like one. The talk of the neighbourhood. Chatter everywhere. Meanwhile, the hand in the window waves and says: Hi, over here - this is me, the caregiver. We're all in physiological and neurological overwhelm. I'm here, trapped, but still willing to say hello. What was that? Oh, that - yes, about that. There isn't a hole big enough for me to bury my head in and hide. This is the reality very few talk about, while others chatter from the outside.

Each condition activates the nervous system in different ways. A short recap explains:

Dementia → confusion, fear, misinterpretation

Triggers emotional reactions that feel sudden and intense.

PTSD → hypervigilance, reactivity, shutdown

Makes the environment feel unsafe, even when it isn't.

Anxiety → constant activation

Keeps everyone on edge, waiting for the next problem.

Together, they create a cycle:

1. Dementia behaviour triggers stress
2. PTSD reacts to the stress
3. Anxiety amplifies the tension
4. The caregiver tries to stabilize everything
5. The caregiver's nerves become overwhelmed
6. The family enters survival mode

This is the perfect storm and the manifestation of a family in chaos. Caregivers often develop PTSD and anxiety along with overwhelm. Regulating everyone all of the time is exhaustive. Whether it begins in childhood or young adulthood, it can be re-activated later due to environmental stressors or develops as something brand new.

Why Caregiving Feels Like Walking Through a Storm

Caregivers in these environments often say:

- "I never know what version of them I'll get."
- "I'm always bracing for something."
- "I can't relax, even for a minute."
- "I feel like I'm constantly putting out fires."
- "I'm tired of being the strong one."
- "I really can't do this anymore.:

- “I am so lost and confused.”
- “It is total darkness.”

These statements are profoundly intense when experienced. They’re accurate descriptions of living in a home where multiple nervous systems are dysregulated at once. These are lived experiences.

Caregiving becomes:

- emotional labour; a burden
- crisis management
- trauma navigation
- constant adaptation
- invisible work
- survival
- a prison

What is unique to caregiving is that the caregiver’s nerves often become the “regulator” for the household until it can’t anymore. This is when things begin to fall apart.

Why Understanding the Storm Matters

You cannot change the storm until you understand its components and begin to clear the chaos.

This chapter helps you see:

- why your home feels chaotic
- why communication breaks down
- why emotions escalate quickly
- why you feel exhausted even on “quiet” days
- why caregiving feels like a full-body experience
- why your nerves are burning out

None of this is imagined. This is systemically very real and very experienced. You are living in a home where multiple members are overwhelmed at the same time.

Let us tread to calm waters. Imagine a crystal-clear blue sea brushing gently against the shoreline - and you right there to welcome it. Feel that, hold it, you are two feet in.

SECTION II - The Breakdown in Families

CHAPTER 4

WHAT A BREAKDOWN REALLY IS

As already mentioned in the previous chapters, most people think of a "breakdown" as a dramatic collapse: crying on the floor, shouting, shaking, or losing control. We've covered it can also be quieter, slower, and far more subtle than people expect. And doesn't always look like a fit. Sometimes, it looks like exhaustion or numbness. Sometimes like irritability, forgetfulness and shutting down or a blank stare. It can be a very long blank stare that can last for hours, at that.

A nervous system breakdown is not a moment, though it does contain moments. It's actually a state of being. It's what happens when the body has been in survival mode for too long and no longer has the capacity to regulate, recover, or return to baseline. It is the circuit board overload, the misfire and burn out.

This chapter aims to help you understand what is actually happening inside the brain and body when someone "breaks," and why. This part is crucial in helping individuals deal with their guilt and shame. It will help create compassion instead of judgement. And God knows, we all could use a little bit of kindness and favour in our lives.

The Nervous System Has Limits

What a thought. Did that ever cross your mind as a caregiver or as an individual, that the nervous system has limits? This is a light bulb moment. Every neurological body has a threshold, a point where it can no longer absorb stress, adapt to pressure, or respond with flexibility. When that threshold is crossed, the system shifts into one of three states:

1. Fight

Irritability, anger, frustration, agitation, emotional intensity.

2. Flight

Restlessness, anxiety, avoidance, overthinking, panic.

3. Freeze/Shutdown

Numbness, exhaustion, disconnection, silence, collapse.

These states are not initial choices because they are automatic biological responses that are hard wired in our body.

As a result, a breakdown happens when the body becomes stuck in one of these states and can't return to balance.

Why Breakdown Happens

Families in chaos live with:

- unpredictable stress
- emotional volatility
- chronic caregiving demands
- sleep disruption
- unresolved trauma

- communication challenges
- sensory overload
- constant vigilance

This creates a perfect environment for breakdown.

When the nervous system is activated repeatedly without enough recovery time, it becomes:

- hypersensitive
- reactive
- easily overwhelmed
- unable to regulate
- unable to rest
- unable to think clearly

This is clear and factual physiological injury.

The Early Signs of Breakdown

Your system will give simple signals it is over loaded with small shifts that are easy to overlook:

- You feel tired even after sleeping.
- You snap at things that never used to bother you.
- You can't focus.
- You feel "on edge" all the time.
- You avoid conversations.
- You feel disconnected from yourself.
- You forget things easily.
- You feel like you're "going through the motions."
- You can't tolerate noise or chaos.

- You feel overwhelmed by simple tasks.

These are early signals.

Your body is saying:
"This is too much."

The Breaking Point

Eventually, your entire body reaches a point where it can no longer compensate. This is the moment families describe as:

- "I can't do this anymore."
- "I feel like I'm losing it."
- "I'm shutting down."
- "I'm feel like exploding."
- "I'm done."

Moments like these can be very charged. They heat up, build and just explode. They can be a few short seconds, or long-drawn-out pyrotechnics.

After the breakdown, eventually when emotions and nerves settle, guilt sets in. The circle loops again, not the path. And you ask yourself, "Why did I say that! I didn't mean to hurt anyone. I am just so maxed." Reality is, how often do we blame the caregiver? After an event like this, a whole load of new stressors enters the family. Completely unwanted or planned. The breakdown happens at the most inconvenient time. No one understands this is not dislike or anger. It isn't a calculated moment. It is caregiver hurt revealed at it's rawest. It is burn out and breakdown all at once.

Another form of breaking down is sobbing uncontrollably or staring at a wall for hours unable to flinch. This happens when someone becomes so overwhelmed, nerves heighten to a point so physically uncomfortable, they crash and numb out so much so, they can not feel, think or move. The nervous system can act like a possum. Play dead when it senses the real threat of danger that someone or something will hurt it.

The breakdown is the body's way of forcing a pause when you've been unable to take one. And it can scream loudly. Your body will do for you what your mind can not. Pause.

What Breakdown Looks Like in Real Life Recap

Breakdown can look like:

Emotional Breakdown

Crying, shaking, panic, overwhelm.

Cognitive Breakdown

Forgetfulness, confusion, inability to make decisions.

Behavioural Breakdown

Withdrawing, isolating, avoiding responsibilities.

Physical Breakdown

Fatigue, headaches, stomach issues, chronic tension.

Relational Breakdown

Irritability, conflict, miscommunication, shutting people out.

Caregiver Breakdown

Feeling resentful, hopeless, or emotionally numb.
These are symptoms an individual has been under too much pressure for too long.

Why Breakdown Feels Like Chaos

When one person breaks, the entire family feels it.

- The caregiver becomes overwhelmed.
- The person with dementia becomes more confused.
- The person with PTSD becomes more reactive.
- The anxious family member becomes more fearful.
- Children become more dysregulated.

This is co-dysregulation.

Families regulate through each other and they dysregulate through each other too.

The Most Important Truth About Breakdown

A breakdown is not the end. It's a message and a signal.

It's the body saying:

- "I need help."
- "I need rest."
- "I need support."
- "I can't carry this alone."

This is the moment you can begin to respond to your body with compassion instead of shame. Through patience and grounding efforts, this period can and will pass and eventually heal.

Where We Go from Here

In the next chapters, we'll explore:

- how breakdown spreads through a family
- why one person's stress becomes everyone's stress
- the patterns that keep families stuck
- how to interrupt the cycle
- how to stabilize the home
- how to support your own nervous system

CHAPTER 5

WHEN ONE PERSON'S STRESS BECOMES EVERYONE'S STRESS

Families function very much like ecosystems. When one part of the system is overwhelmed, the entire system shifts to adapt.

In chaos, this process happens quickly and rather intensely. The ripple affect can get really out of control when one person's stress becomes everyone's stress. As I have explained thus far; nerves are wired to respond to the emotional states around them.

This chapter explains why tension spreads so easily and conflict escalates just as fast, and why even the smallest of stressors can ripple and fall like a house of cards.

Stress Is Contagious, Literally

The central nervous system is constantly scanning the environment for cues of safety or danger. It does this through:

- facial expressions
- tone of voice
- body language
- breathing patterns
- pacing
- emotional energy

When someone in the home becomes stressed, they send out signals, often without a single word being spoken. Others pick up on those signals instantly.

This is why:

- a sigh can change the mood
- a raised voice can shift the atmosphere
- a tense posture can make the room feel unsafe
- a shutdown can make others feel abandoned
- a panic response can trigger more panic
- walking away can feel like dismissal, arrogance, or disrespect

Your body responds before your mind even understands what's happening.

Co-Regulation and Co-Dysregulation

Humans are designed to co-regulate and calm each other through connection.
But when stress is high, families often co-dysregulate instead.

Co-Regulation

Two nervous systems syncing into calm.

Co-Dysregulation

Two nervous systems syncing into chaos.

In chaos, co-dysregulation happens easily because:

- the baseline stress level is already high
- the window of tolerance is smaller

- triggers are more frequent
- emotional reserves are lower
- sleep is disrupted
- communication is strained

This is why a single moment of tension can turn into a full-house meltdown. Something totally unexpected, completely unexplainable and without any notice.

The Roles People Fall into Under Stress

When stress spreads, family members often fall into predictable roles because of a default to survival patterns.

1. The Fixer

Tries to calm everyone, solve everything, and prevent conflict.
Often the caregiver.

2. The Exploder

Releases stress outward through anger or intensity.
Often misunderstood as "the problem."

3. The Withdrawer

Shuts down, goes quiet, or disappears emotionally.
Often seen as "not helping."

4. The Absorber

Takes on everyone else's emotions.
Often the most exhausted.

5. The Avoider

Distracts, escapes, or numbs.
Often coping with more than they can express.

It is fundamentally important to acknowledge that these roles are not necessarily the personality trait or character of a person. They are strategies the individual creates very early on to survive and cope. They can also blend and become hybrid roles for survival.

Why Caregivers Feel It the Most

Caregivers often become the emotional anchor of the home and the whole family emotionally depends on them. Their empathy and compassion make them very open.

They absorb:

- dementia behaviors
- PTSD reactions
- anxiety spirals
- emotional outbursts
- shutdowns
- confusion
- fear
- responsibility

This ability to relieve others by absorbing behaviours and outcomes can become toxic as the neuron's communication labour amplifies and reacts with the emotional labour.

How Stress Spreads in Dementia, PTSD, and Anxiety

Each condition amplifies the others.

Dementia

Creates confusion → triggers fear → increases tension.

PTSD

Creates hypervigilance → triggers reactivity → increases conflict.

Anxiety

Creates constant activation → triggers overwhelm → increases emotional sensitivity.

Together, they create a cycle where:

1. One person becomes overwhelmed
2. Another reacts to the overwhelm
3. Another absorbs the reaction
4. Another shuts down
5. The caregiver tries to stabilize everything
6. The caregiver becomes overwhelmed
7. The cycle repeats

This chain reaction is the friction behind family chaos.

And it Feels Personal

When someone reacts strongly, shuts down, or lashes out, it's easy to interpret it as:

- disrespect
- rejection
- anger
- lack of appreciation
- intentional behavior
- judgement

But most of the time, it's none of those things as it is that person's neurological coping response to a circumstance or crisis.

Understanding this doesn't excuse harmful behaviour but it helps explain it. This also helps to identify it, a first step toward diffusing the emotional response by halting it from being damaging and personal to your own sense of self.

The First Step Toward Breaking the Cycle

You cannot stop stress from entering or it becoming dysfunctional chaos.
But you *can* stop it from spreading.

The first step is recognizing:

- what belongs to you
- what belongs to someone else
- what belongs to the neurological body
- what belongs to the environment
- what belongs to the pattern

When you see the pattern, you can stop it and say, not now, not today. Immunize it however necessary; however, it speaks to you without going to extremes. Stop it dead in its transmission.

When you can contain it, this is the beginning of actionable support. This chapter gave you the foundation.

The next chapter shows you the patterns that keep families stuck and how to begin shifting away from them for good. Rebuild new patterns you do want to keep and fortify them.

CHAPTER 6

THE PATTERNS THAT KEEP FAMILIES IN CHAOS

Chaos is a state of complete overwhelm.

When stress becomes chronic, trauma builds up and shapes communication. Sometimes it can be in the shape of victim dialogue; dialogue that is crying out for help and never getting it, where there is deep emotional active hurt. You can feel it. Or sometimes the dialogue can be abrupt from the individual who is saturated; always having to be the responsible one. Where the hurt is pushed aside or deep down, and there is not active recognition of pain, just a huge auto function to do. There can be other variants; a kaleidoscope of traits behind the expression of trauma. When dementia, PTSD or anxiety is part of daily life, families begin to operate in predictable patterns. Spotting these patterns is the key to dissolving them and breaking the adaptation.

And like all adaptations, they make sense in the moment... even when they create long term strain. This is the reason they continue to exist. But this is also the auto-pilot mode. My goal is to get us out of auto-pilot. It worked for a time. But now, let's re-engage and steer this plane home. And land safely!

These patterns keep families stuck, let's recognize them so you can begin to shift them with clarity and compassion.

Pattern 1: Over-functioning and Under-functioning

When there is trauma at home, roles often polarize.

The Over-Doer

- anticipates everyone's needs
- manages the emotional climate
- takes on extra responsibilities
- tries to prevent conflict
- becomes the "strong one"

The Under-Doer

- withdraws
- avoids decisions
- becomes overwhelmed easily
- shuts down under pressure
- relies heavily on the over-doer

Let's remember again that these roles are not personality traits but pre-programmed nervous system responses.

The over-doer's system says:

"If I don't hold everything together, everything will fall apart."

The underdoer's system says:

"I can't handle more. I need to retreat."

Both are survival strategies that are valid, but also create imbalance.

Pattern 2: The Caregiver Guilt Loop

Caregivers often live in a cycle of:

1. Doing everything

2. Feeling exhausted

3. Feeling guilty for being exhausted

4. Pushing harder

5. Becoming more overwhelmed

6. Feeling guilty again

This loop is fueled by:

- unrealistic expectations
- cultural pressure
- family history
- trauma conditioning
- fear of letting someone down
- fear of being judged
- fear of not being enough

The guilt loop keeps caregivers from resting, asking for help, or setting boundaries which only deepens the chaos.

Pattern 3: Avoidance and Explosion

When emotions feel too big, families often swing between two extremes:

Avoidance

- not talking about problems
- minimizing issues
- pretending things are fine
- walking on eggshells
- suppressing feelings

Explosion

- sudden arguments
- emotional outbursts
- intense reactions
- conflict that feels disproportionate

Avoidance builds pressure. Explosion releases it. Then the cycle starts again. But with each cycle that starts again, there is a weakening of the individual nervous system and as a result the family as a whole as well.

This is not immaturity or insanity. Though our rational mind wants to call it something. Factually, this is dis-regulation.

Pattern 4: The "Fixer" and the "Triggered"

In many families, one person becomes the fixer: the one who smooths things over, calms everyone down, and tries to plainly resolve it.

Another person becomes the triggered one: the one whose nervous system reacts quickly, intensely, or unpredictably.

And sometimes, one person can be both!

They are usually shaped by:

- trauma history
- brain changes
- emotional capacity
- chronic stress
- caregiving demands

The fixer feels responsible. The triggered person feels overwhelmed. Both feel misunderstood. And sometimes, as the family evolves and expands, roles can interweave and become both or a hybrid version.

Pattern 5: Silence as Safety

Silence often becomes a survival strategy.

People stop sharing their needs because:

- they don't want to burden others
- they fear conflict
- they don't want to trigger someone
- they're too tired to explain
- they've learned that speaking up leads to tension

Silence feels safer than honesty. But silence also creates distance; coldness and a lot of buried resentment that can take a lifetime to heal. Coldness further creates disinterest and apathy! This sword is a dangerous one. Here guilt does not have an active expression. It is either buried or cut off. Here, you risk disassociation from the family and no remorse. An example is God syndrome or isolation; an 'I do not need anyone' attitude can develop.

Pattern 6: Crisis Based Connection

Some families only come together during:

- medical emergencies
- emotional breakdowns
- behavioral escalations
- moments of fear
- moments of chaos
- moments of loss

Crisis becomes the glue. Calm feels unfamiliar. Peace feels suspicious.

This happens when families have learned to bond through urgency. This is not that families love drama or chaos. It is because these circumstances bring them together and deep down, the family unit does want to be together even though they survive differently.

Pattern 7: Emotional Mismatching

In overwhelmed families, people often operate in different emotional states at the same time:

- one person is anxious
- one person is numb
- one person is angry
- one person is confused
- one person is trying to fix everything

These mismatched states create misunderstandings:

- The anxious person feels ignored.
- The numb person feels pressured.
- The angry person feels provoked.
- The confused person feels lost.
- The fixer feels alone.

No one is wrong. They're just in different nervous states.

Why These Patterns Feel Impossible to Break

Patterns persist because:

- the body defaults to what feels familiar
- stress reduces flexibility
- trauma reduces emotional capacity
- caregiving reduces energy
- families adapt to survive, not to thrive

You cannot change a pattern while you're still inside survival mode.

This is why families often say:

- "We keep having the same argument."
- "Nothing ever changes."
- "We're stuck."
- "I don't know how to break this cycle."

The First Step Toward Change

The best way to shift a pattern is through choice and through awareness. And with courage.

Seeing the pattern gives you the conscious choice to break it. When you identify it in your mind, you can soften its hold. This is the beginning of the shift to change; to take action from a conscious state of seeing.

The next chapter gives you the tools to assist you in making a change.

CHAPTER 7

HOW TO INTERRUPT THE BREAKDOWN CYCLE

In my experience, families don't want to live in chaos. They want to be happy. They want ease, connection, and peace. Of course, there are exceptions - there always are - but most families are simply doing their best inside circumstances that overwhelm them.

Usually, chaos remains because no one is shown how to interrupt the cycle that perpetuates the chaos. And sometimes, the fear of change is so strong, even when it is named, it can be denied due to the gripping fear.

When nervous systems are overwhelmed, people react. They don't always choose their tone or their shutdown; or panic, or anger, withdrawal, or confusion. These are fast, instinctive, and deeply wired survival responses.

The good news is with commitment and attention; cycles can be interrupted.
Patterns can be reduced. Breakdowns can be slowed. Chaos can be contained to eventually one day be completely dissolved. We are not on a timer. We are on a journey. This is a process that takes as long as is needed. No one can give you an expiration date on change.

By understanding what your intricate nervous system needs in the very moment you begin to spiral, you can start nudging the family dynamic back toward joy, love, peace, and comfort. You bring nurture and care home. Oh, what was that? Anxiety and embarrassment have to leave? Sure - no problem. I'll gladly walk them out the door. Bye-bye.

Let's look at how.

Step 1: Recognize the Early Warning Signs

The subtle cues the body whispers before it screams.

Early signs include:

- shorter fuse
- shallow breathing
- pacing
- withdrawing
- talking faster
- going quiet
- feeling overwhelmed by small tasks
- rising tension in the room
- confusion or forgetfulness
- a sudden shift in tone

When you learn to notice these early cues, you can intervene before the spiral takes over.

This is not about controlling someone else. It's about understanding neurological language.

Step 2: Slow the Pace of the Moment

Chaos accelerates. Your job is to slow it down.

You can interrupt the cycle by:

- lowering your voice
- speaking fewer words
- pausing before responding

- softening your facial expression
- reducing movement in the room
- stepping back physically
- giving more space
- removing extra stimuli (noise, lights, clutter)

Slowing the pace signals safety. Safety signals regulation.

Step 3: Shift From Logic to Physiology

In a breakdown, the thinking brain goes offline. And the survival brain takes over.

This means:

- explanations won't work
- reasoning won't work
- reminders won't work
- logic won't work
- "Calm down" definitely won't work

Instead, shift to physiological support:

- grounding
- orienting
- breathing together
- reducing sensory input
- offering a simple, concrete choice
- using a calm, steady tone

Remember, you're not trying to win an argument. You're trying to help a nervous body feel safe enough to come back online.

Step 4: Contain the Stress, Don't Absorb It

Caregivers often absorb everyone else's emotions.
This is how they burn out.

Containment is different from absorption.

Absorption

"I feel what you feel."

Containment

"I see what you feel, and I can stay steady while you feel it."

Containment looks like:

- grounding yourself before responding
- keeping your tone steady
- not matching the other person's intensity
- not taking their reaction personally
- not escalating to meet their escalation

Containment interrupts the cycle because it prevents co-dysregulation.

Step 5: Use Micro-Interventions

You don't need big tools.
You need small, repeatable ones.

Micro-interventions include:

- "Let's take a breath together."
- "I'm here."
- "One thing at a time."
- "Let's pause for a moment."

- "We can come back to this."
- "Let's sit down."
- "Let's step outside for a minute."

These tiny shifts create space and space interrupts spirals.

Step 6: Reduce the Sensory Load

Overwhelm is often sensory, not emotional.

You can interrupt a breakdown by reducing:

- noise
- movement
- lights
- clutter
- competing conversations
- background stimulation

A calmer environment creates a calmer nervous system.

Step 7: Step Out of the Cycle When Needed

Sometimes the most powerful intervention is stepping away.

Not abandoning.
Not punishing.
Not withdrawing in anger.

Stepping away with a clear intention:

- "I'm going to take a moment so we don't escalate."
- "I'll be right back."
- "Let's pause and breathe separately."

This prevents the cycle from feeding itself.

Step 8: Repair After the Storm

Interrupting the cycle is only half the work.
Repair is the other half.

Repair looks like:

- acknowledging the moment
- validating the feelings
- clarifying misunderstandings
- reconnecting gently
- offering reassurance
- naming what went well
- naming what can change next time

Repair teaches that conflict is survivable — and that connection can return.

Why These Steps Work

These steps work because they:

- reduce activation
- increase safety
- slow the pace
- support regulation
- prevent escalation
- create predictability
- build trust
- strengthen connection

This step creates a shift by supporting the central nervous system. And by not stopping the emotion but by interrupting the spiral.

You're not preventing stress from happening but you're preventing it from spreading.

The Most Important Truth

Interrupting the breakdown cycle is not about perfection. It's about presence.

It's about learning to recognize:

- "This is a nervous moment."
- "This is not personal."
- "This is not my fault."
- "This is not their fault."
- "We can slow this down."

The key thing to remember here is that you don't need to control the storm itself, you just need to anchor yourself long enough to change its direction.

SECTION III - Tools for Stability and Support

CHAPTER 8

CRISIS TOOLS THAT ACTUALLY HELP

When a family is overwhelmed, the hardest moments are the ones that feel like they come out of nowhere: the sudden outburst, the panic spike, the confusion, the shutdown, the argument that escalates too fast, the moment when the person you love becomes unreachable.

Most families try to respond with logic, explanations, or problem-solving. Which many times just makes things unsettled or leaves things fractured. Also, remember that in crisis, the thinking brain is offline.

Crisis is not a communication problem. Though the external seems to be this way. Systemically, it goes back to it being one's nerves.

This next chapter gives you tools that work in the moment. Tools that don't require calm, cooperation, or perfect timing. These tools support the body first because the body is where crisis lives.

They are techniques and not complicated. They are simple, repeatable, and physiological. They work because they meet the nervous system where it is.

Tool 1: Grounding - Bringing the Body Back into the Present

When someone is overwhelmed, they are either:

- stuck in the past (trauma memory)
- stuck in the future (fear of what's coming)
- or stuck in survival mode (fight/flight/freeze)

Grounding brings them back to the present moment.

How to use it in crisis:

- Speak slowly
- Use simple, concrete language
- Bring attention to the senses

Examples:

- "Feel your feet on the floor."
- "Look at me for a second."
- "Can you hold this object?"
- "Let's take one slow breath together."

Grounding interrupts the spiral by giving something real to hold onto.

Tool 2: Orienting - Helping the Brain Re-Establish Safety

When someone is overwhelmed, their brain loses track of context. They forget:

- where they are
- who is with them
- what is happening
- whether they are safe
- what day it is

Orienting restores that context.

How to use it:

- Gently draw attention to the environment
- Use calm, factual statements
- Avoid questions that require thinking

Examples:

- "You're here with me."
- "We're in the living room."
- "You're safe right now."
- "Nothing bad is happening in this moment."

This is especially powerful for dementia, PTSD, and panic.

Tool 3: Breathwork That Doesn't Trigger Panic

Traditional deep breathing can make anxiety worse.
People feel trapped, pressured, or suffocated.

Instead, use **exhale-focused breathing**, which activates the parasympathetic (calming) system.

How to use it:

- "Let's breathe out slowly together."
- "Long exhale... short inhale."
- "Blow the air out like you're cooling soup."

This works because the exhale is what signals safety to the body.

Tool 4: The One-Thing Rule

In crisis, the brain cannot handle multiple instructions.
It can barely handle one.

The One-Thing Rule simplifies the moment.

How to use it:

Give one clear, concrete action:

- "Sit with me."
- "Hold my hand."
- "Let's step outside."
- "Drink this water."
- "Put your feet on the ground."

One thing. Not three. Not five. One.

This reduces overwhelm instantly.

Tool 5: The Softening Technique

Your tone is more important than your words.

A soft tone:

- lowers activation
- reduces defensiveness
- signals safety
- slows the pace of the moment

Softening looks like:

- lowering your voice
- slowing your speech
- relaxing your shoulders
- softening your face
- reducing movement

You become the regulated anchor in the room.

Tool 6: The 10-Second Pause

When crisis escalates, speed is the enemy.

A 10-second pause:

- interrupts the automatic reaction
- gives your nervous system a moment to settle
- prevents co-dysregulation
- slows the entire interaction

You can say:

- "Let's pause for a moment."
- "Give me a second."
- "I'm taking a breath."

This tiny pause can prevent a full spiral.

Tool 7: Environmental Reset

Sometimes the fastest way to calm the nerves is to change the environment.

Suggestions on how to do this:

- turn off the TV
- dim the lights
- reduce noise
- open a window
- step outside
- move to a quieter room

The body responds to the environment before it responds to words.

Tool 8: The "I'm Here" Anchor

In crisis, people often feel alone, even if you're standing right beside them.

A simple, steady phrase can anchor them:

- "I'm here."
- "I'm with you."
- "You're not alone."
- "You are safe."

This is especially powerful for dementia and PTSD.

It doesn't fix the crisis but stabilizes their nerves so the crisis can pass.

Tool 9: The Micro-Choice Technique

Choice restores control. Control restores safety.

But choices must be stay simple to be effective.

How to use it:

- "Do you want to sit or stand?"

- "Do you want water or tea?"
- "Do you want to stay here or move to the couch?"

Micro-choices reduce overwhelm and increase regulation. This also gives the person in crisis choice, which at the time of crisis, the person believes they do not have.

Tool 10: The After-Crisis Reset

After the moment passes, the nerves and full nervous system need a reset.

This reset can be:

- a walk
- a warm drink
- a quiet room
- a weighted blanket
- a few minutes of silence
- a grounding object

This helps the body return to baseline so the next crisis is less likely.

Why These Tools Work

They work because they:

- reduce activation
- increase safety
- simplify the moment
- support physiology
- prevent escalation
- create predictability
- restore connection

You're not trying to fix the crisis. You're giving support so your loved one gets through it.

You are also not trying to control the other person; you're providing a feeling of safety, just enough for them to come back to themselves.

These were your practical toolkit. The next chapter builds on them by teaching you how to communicate in ways that reduce conflict and increase connection.

CHAPTER 9

COMMUNICATION THAT REDUCES CONFLICT

We all know that without communication, collective interaction as the world knows it would be close to impossible. Most families believe their communication problems come from misunderstandings, personality differences, or "not being on the same page." But in trauma, dementia-impacted, or anxiety within homes, communication challenges are rarely about words.

When someone is overwhelmed, confused, triggered, or dysregulated, they cannot hear tone accurately or process complex sentences. They also find it very difficult to follow long explanations. And importantly, they cannot access empathy or perspective-taking because they completely lack grounding.

Communication that reduces conflict begins with understanding what the nervous system can and cannot do under stress.

This chapter gives you tools that help you speak in ways that soothe, connect and support the individual or family.

Why Traditional Communication Fails in Trauma Induced Families

Most communication advice assumes:

- both people are calm
- both people can think clearly
- both people can access empathy

- both people can regulate their emotions
- both people can tolerate discomfort

In previous chapters we know:

Dementia affects memory and comprehension.
PTSD affects threat perception.
Anxiety affects tone interpretation.
Caregiver burnout affects patience and clarity.

Traditional communication fails because it relies on the thinking brain and the thinking brain is often offline.

You need communication that works with the body, not against it.

THE FOUNDATIONS OF TRAUMA-INFORMED COMMUNICATION

1. Speak to the Body First, the Mind Second

When someone is dysregulated, their body needs safety before their mind can analyze.

This means:

- slow your voice
- soften your tone
- reduce your volume
- pause between sentences
- use fewer words
- keep your body still

Your nervous system activates the message.

2. Use Short, Simple Sentences

Long explanations overwhelm the brain.

Instead of:

"Can you please stop raising your voice, because it's making me uncomfortable and I'm trying to have a calm conversation with you."

Try:

"Let's slow down."
"I'm right here."
"One thing at a time."
"Let's take a breath."

Short sentences reduce cognitive load and prevent escalation.

3. Remove Blame from Your Language

Blame activates defensiveness.
Defensiveness activates the survival brain.
The survival brain activates conflict.

Shift from:

"You never listen."
"You're overreacting."
"You're confusing me."
"You're making this harder."

To:

"Let's try this together."
"I want to understand."

"Let's slow down."
"We can figure this out."

This keeps the conversation in the window of tolerance.

4. Validate Before You Redirect

Validation does not mean agreement.
It means acknowledgment.

Validation sounds like:

"I see this is hard."
"It makes sense you're overwhelmed."
"I hear you."
"I get why you're upset."

Validation calms the nervous system enough to allow redirection.

5. Use Predictable Phrases

Predictability creates safety.

Choose a few phrases you use consistently:

- "I'm right here."
- "We're okay."
- "Let's pause."
- "One thing at a time."
- "We'll figure this out."

These become anchors during stress.

6. Avoid "Why" Questions

"Why" requires reflection, something the survival brain cannot do.

Instead of:

"Why are you upset?"
"Why did you do that?"
"Why can't you calm down?"

Try:

"What's happening right now?"
"What do you need?"
"What's the next step?"
"What would help?"

"What" keeps the brain in the present moment. "Why makes it think deeper and right now, in crisis mode, it cannot think deeper."

7. Match the Emotional Intensity, Then Lower It

If someone is extremely activated, responding with extreme calm can feel dismissive.

Instead:

- match their intensity for one sentence
- then slowly lower yours

Example:

"I hear you, this is a lot."
"Let's slow down."
"We can take this one step at a time."

This creates a bridge between states.

8. Use Gentle Redirection Instead of Correction

Correction triggers shame.
Shame triggers defensiveness.
Defensiveness triggers escalation.

Instead of:

"That's not what happened."
"You're remembering wrong."
"You're being dramatic."

Try:

"Let's look at this together."
"Here's what I remember."
"Let's take a moment."

This preserves dignity and connection.

9. Know When to Pause the Conversation

You cannot communicate through a shutdown or a panic spike.

Pausing is not avoidance. Pausing can be a form of regulation.

You can say:

"Let's take a moment."
"I need a breath."
"We can come back to this."
"Let's pause so we don't escalate."

A regulated pause prevents a full spiral.

10. Repair After Miscommunication

Repair is the most important part of communication.

Repair sounds like:

"I didn't mean to escalate things."
"I'm sorry for my tone."
"Let's try again."
"I care about you."
"We're on the same team."

Repair teaches the nervous system and the brain that conflict is survivable.

Why These Tools Work

They work because they:

- reduce activation
- increase safety
- simplify the moment
- prevent escalation
- support connection
- honor dignity
- create predictability
- strengthen trust

You're not trying to win the conversation but protect the relationship and regulate the moment. You are also not trying to avoid the moment to prevent unnecessary pain. This shift in perception matters because it allows for the first step.

This is "the communication foundation".

The next chapter expands into **regulation for the whole family**, so the home itself becomes a calmer, safer place.

CHAPTER 10
REGULATION FOR THE WHOLE FAMILY

Contrary to popular thinking and though genetically correct, family is not just a collection of DNA bonded individuals. A family is also a network or a community or a close circle or a unit not necessarily connected via DNA.

We all now know, that when one person becomes overwhelmed, the entire circle feels it.
When one person calms, the entire circle benefits.

Regulation is a necessity in balanced functioning. It is about creating conditions where calm becomes possible. And also, when amidst chaos becomes the responsible pivot.

This chapter teaches you how to build a home environment that supports regulation not just for the person with dementia, PTSD, or anxiety, but for everyone in the household, including you! (Caregiver or not)!

This will be about rhythm, predictability, and small daily practices that slowly shift the emotional climate of the home.

THE FOUNDATIONS OF FAMILY REGULATION

1. Predictability Creates Safety

Nerves love predictability. It reduces threat perception and increases emotional capacity.

Predictability can be created through:

- consistent routines
- clear expectations
- simple daily rhythms
- predictable transitions
- familiar cues

Examples:

- morning routine that doesn't change
- consistent mealtimes
- a predictable bedtime flow
- a "quiet hour" in the evening
- a daily walk
- a calming ritual before difficult tasks

Predictability doesn't eliminate stress but reduces the nervous system's workload.

2. The Home Environment Matters More Than You Think

A regulated home is not a quiet home. It's a supported home.

Small environmental shifts can dramatically reduce overwhelm:

- reduce clutter
- lower background noise
- use warm lighting
- create a calm corner

- keep pathways clear
- reduce competing stimuli (TV + conversation + movement)
- use soft textures and grounding objects

The environment communicates safety before words do. Remember, the environment first creates the space and then the body reacts to it.

3. Regulation Is a Shared Responsibility

This is one of my favourite truths! Team effort wins every time! How satisfying as well, for everyone. In trauma active families, one person often becomes the emotional anchor. This is however, unsustainable.

Regulation becomes easier when:

- everyone has tools
- everyone understands their own triggers
- everyone knows how to pause
- everyone practices grounding
- everyone participates in routines

Caregivers please remember: You are not responsible for regulating everyone, but can be effective in creating the scenario where everyone participates in their own self-regulation. How truly wonderful, my dream environment!

4. Build Micro-Regulation into the Day

It happens in small, repeated actions. These are often the most effective.

Micro-regulation practices include:

- 30-second breathing breaks
- grounding before transitions
- stretching together

- stepping outside for fresh air
- drinking water
- brief silence
- sensory resets (warm drink, cool cloth, weighted blanket)

These tiny practices prevent the nervous system from accumulating stress. And let's face it, no one wants more cortisol rising in their body. We know our adrenals need a break.

5. Create a Family Regulation Language

Families need shared words for shared experiences.

Examples:

- "I need a pause."
- "My body feels tight."
- "I'm getting overwhelmed."
- "Let's slow down."
- "I need space."
- "Can we reset?"

This language normalizes regulation.

6. Teach Children Regulation Through Modeling

It has been proven through research that children learn best when experiencing the thing they are learning. As an example:

- watching you breathe
- watching you pause
- watching you repair

- watching you soften
- watching you name your feelings
- watching you take breaks

Your regulation becomes their template. And they start to repeat the same function response. Some call it mimicking, I prefer it as learning how to take new steps. Children idolize their elders. It would make sense they learn from them by repeating their movements.

7. Use Co-Regulation Intentionally

Co-regulation is the natural way of calming through connection.

You can co-regulate by:

- sitting close
- offering a hand
- matching breathing
- using a soft tone
- slowing your movements
- offering grounding objects
- using gentle touch (if welcomed)

Co-regulation is a form of anchoring.

8. Create a "Calm Plan" for the Household

A calm plan is a simple, predictable set of steps the family uses when tension rises.

It might include:

- a phrase everyone recognizes ("Let's reset")
- a pause
- grounding
- moving to a quieter space
- reducing sensory input
- a short walk
- a drink of water
- a moment of silence

A calm plan prevents escalation by giving the family a shared roadmap.

9. Normalize Rest

Rest is regulation. Please remember this. So very effective when practiced.

Families often resist rest because:

- they feel guilty
- they feel behind
- they feel responsible
- they feel unsafe slowing down
- they've learned to survive through productivity

Did you know that rest is how the nervous system repairs itself.

Normalize:

- naps
- quiet time
- early bedtimes
- breaks
- doing nothing

- stepping away
- saying "I need a moment"

Rest is a very needed medicine! So please, take it.

10. Celebrate Small Moments of Regulation

Regulation grows when you notice what went right.

Celebrate:

- a calm conversation
- a shorter argument
- a successful pause
- a moment of connection
- a shared laugh
- a gentle repair
- a quiet evening

They are signs of healing. Celebrate them. Encourage them.

Why Family Regulation Matters

Regulation is the foundation of:

- communication
- connection
- problem-solving
- emotional safety
- resilience

- healing

A regulated family is a family that can return to safety after stress.

These are the daily practices you can use to create balance.
The next chapter helps you understand **your own nervous system as a caregiver**, so you can support others without losing yourself.

SECTION IV - Caring for Yourself Without Losing Yourself

CHAPTER 11

THE CAREGIVER'S NEUROLOGY

Caregivers are often the emotional backbone of the family. They absorb the stress, soften the edges, anticipate needs, prevent conflict, and hold the household together when everything feels like it's falling apart.

But caregivers are not superhuman. They are not immune to overwhelm or built to carry endless emotional weight without support.

Caregivers have nerves that need attention too and those nerves are often pushed far beyond their limits.

This chapter will help you understand your own internal landscape, the full load you carry, and why caregiving affects your body, mind, and emotions so deeply.

THE INVISIBLE REALITY OF CAREGIVER STRESS

Most caregivers don't realize how overwhelmed they are until something breaks:

- patience

- sleep
- memory
- mood
- health
- hope

Caregiver stress is really cumulative. It builds slowly, quietly, and consistently.

Burn out isn't a result of one bad day. It is because of hundreds, maybe thousands of days where you kept going anyway.

Compassion Fatigue: When Caring Becomes a Burden

Compassion fatigue or empathy burn out is the exhaustion that comes from caring deeply for too long without enough replenishment. It is the dry out when your heart can't give love in the moment anymore because your nervous system is so depleted it is dry. I know this phase all too well. As a Personal Coach and caregiver helping to run multiple households and attend to the emotional needs of my clients as well; compassion and empathy burn out was in fact my extreme reality. It was a sudden emotional taxation of years of overload. And I felt it, in every possible way.

This juncture when reached becomes a very pivotal moment in someone's life. It is the awakening of now or never. Either we rest, we take stock, we replenish or we burn out for good. Which can happen. And sometimes is the survival default. At this point, we are beyond just offline. We are now the server that has crashed. Systems down. Here, we need much more than a reset or a reboot. We need a whole new system repair.

Signs of burn out fatigue include:

- emotional numbness
- irritability
- feeling detached
- feeling guilty for feeling detached
- reduced empathy
- feeling "done" even when you don't want to be

Compassion fatigue is not failing. Though there is a heavy burden when you can not give effortlessly as before. Compassion fatigue is a signal that there is no more energy to input for the output.

2. Hypervigilance: Living in Anticipation Mode

In many circumstances, over many experiences, caregivers often default to live in a constant state of readiness:

- waiting for the next behavior
- anticipating the next need
- bracing for the next outburst
- listening for movement at night
- watching for signs of confusion or distress

This is hypervigilance where the nervous system is stuck in "alert mode."

This states often leads to:

- exhaustion
- anxiety
- irritability
- difficulty relaxing
- trouble sleeping

- feeling “on edge” all the time

Hypervigilance is different from paranoia. It is a trauma response.

The key difference lies in the belief: hypervigilance is always about anticipating the future threat. Whilst paranoia involves beliefs about current threats.

3. Emotional Numbing: The Body’s Last-Resort Protection

When the nervous system is overwhelmed for too long, it shuts down emotional intensity to protect itself.

This can look like:

- feeling disconnected
- going through the motions
- losing interest in things you used to enjoy
- feeling like you’re watching your life instead of living it
- struggling to feel joy

Numbing is not apathy. It’s survival. Apathy is often the long-term affliction that results from numbing. It becomes a chronic state or shape of one’s expression. Numbing could become apathy if neglected.

4. Cognitive Fatigue: When Your Brain Can’t Keep Up

Caregivers often describe:

- forgetfulness
- difficulty concentrating
- trouble making decisions

- mental fog
- feeling scattered
- losing track of time

If I can make a very valuable suggestion here: it is best to see this not as a personal flaw or a sign of aging. It's really about cognitive overload. Your brain is just juggling too much. It can no longer process effectively. I have learned that through pause, practice and new methodologies, your cognitive brain function can be restored to a level of pre-overwhelm and even 20 years before. There is a lot of research out there for this type of healing. It requires daily change.

5. The Loss of Self: When Caregiving Takes Over Your Identity

Many caregivers reach a point where they have truly abandoned their needs to a point where they say:

- "I don't know who I am anymore."
- "My whole life revolves around caregiving."
- "I've lost myself."

This happens because:

- your needs get pushed aside
- your routines disappear
- your hobbies fade
- your friendships shrink
- your dreams get postponed
- your nervous system is always in service mode

Losing yourself is the cost of chronic responsibility and sacrifice of your time.

WHY CAREGIVERS BREAK DOWN

Caregivers break down because:

- they carry too much
- they rest too little
- they feel responsible for everything
- they don't want to burden others
- they don't feel allowed to ask for help
- they feel guilty for needing anything
- they believe they should be stronger
- Their sense of loyalty over-rides all else

Caregivers do shoulder far more than is normal.

THE CAREGIVER'S NERVES NEED CARE TOO

Your nervous system needs:

- rest
- boundaries
- support
- validation
- breaks
- nourishment
- connection
- compassion

These are necessities. You cannot regulate others if you are chronically dysregulated or anchor the home if you are sinking!

This chapter is about recognition, value and the commitment to implement self-care.

So please practice care as well. Whether you are a family caregiver, a professional caregiver, a spiritual caregiver, a coach or combination of 2 or more of these hybrid identities. Everyone deserves support, rest, respite, and care.

This next section is about the why behind certain behaviours that keep you looping:

- why you over-function
- why you feel responsible for everything
- why you struggle to rest
- why you carry guilt
- why you silence your needs
- why you push past your limits

And most importantly, how to begin reclaiming yourself.

CHAPTER 12

HEALING YOUR OWN PATTERNS

In Chapter 6 we saw how these patterns play out across a family — now let's look at the ones you carry personally.

If we take time to observe, we can spot patterns in behaviours. We can spot it in everything really. And caregiving, patterns are exposed by:

The ways you respond under pressure.
The ways you protect yourself.
The ways you try to keep the peace.
The ways you silence your needs.
The ways you overextend.
The ways you disappear into responsibility.

These patterns began before caregiving. They were shaped by your childhood, your relationships, your trauma history, the development and state of your nervous system, and the environments you've survived.

Caregiving simply magnifies them to repeat themselves with stronger impact.

This chapter will help you understand your patterns with compassion to begin to slow and heal them.

THE PATTERNS CAREGIVERS CARRY

1. The Over-functioning Pattern

Over-functioning is the belief that:

- "If I don't do it, it won't get done."
- "If I rest, everything will fall apart."
- "I have to be the strong one."
- "Everyone depends on me."

Over-functioning looks like:

- doing more than your share
- anticipating everyone's needs
- taking responsibility for others' emotions
- preventing conflict
- never resting
- never asking for help

This pattern often forms in childhood when you had to grow up too fast or take care of others before taking care of yourself. It may have been to over compensate another family member who just wouldn't do it. So, you did!

Over-functioning is a survival mode. But now, you can choose differently. Pat yourself on the back for your hard-core discipline and deep compassion for getting things done when no one else would do it. But now, this is a chance to view the scenario from a new perspective of choice in mind, not survival.

2. The Self-Silencing Pattern

Self-silencing is the habit of pushing your needs aside because:

- you don't want to burden anyone
- you fear conflict

- you feel guilty for needing anything
- you've learned your needs don't matter
- you're used to being the "pleasing one"

Self-silencing looks like:

- saying "I'm fine" when you're not
- hiding your exhaustion
- avoiding asking for help
- minimizing your feelings
- prioritizing others at your own expense

This pattern forms when your nervous system learns that speaking up leads to pain, rejection, or conflict.

Self-silencing is more an act of self-abandonment than peace making

It makes you feel invisible to the rest of the world and your family.

3. The Hyper-Responsibility Pattern

Hyper-responsibility is the belief that you are responsible for:

- everyone's emotions
- everyone's safety
- everyone's comfort
- everyone's stability
- everyone's reactions

This pattern forms when you grew up in unpredictable environments where you had to manage the emotional climate to stay safe.

Hyper-responsibility is more related to fear than self-care.

4. The Guilt-Driven Pattern

Caregivers often carry guilt like a second skin.

Guilt for:

- not doing enough
- doing too much
- feeling tired
- feeling resentful
- wanting a break
- wanting your life back
- not being perfect
- being human

This guilt is neurological — the result of chronic stress and unrealistic expectations. And personalized pain. This is when caring can really, really hurt.

Guilt is a signal.

5. The Emotional Numbing Pattern

Emotional numbing is a result of a system that has been overwhelmed for too long: your nervous system protects you by numbing your emotions.

Numbing looks like:

- going through the motions
- feeling disconnected
- losing interest in things you used to enjoy

- feeling like you're watching your life from the outside
- struggling to feel joy

Numbing is an extreme expression of exhaustion.

WHY THESE PATTERNS FORM

These patterns form because:

- you learned to survive by being useful
- you learned to stay safe by staying quiet
- you learned to avoid conflict by over-functioning
- you learned to earn love through self-sacrifice
- you learned that your needs were secondary
- you learned that rest was dangerous
- you learned that responsibility equals worth

They are adaptations. And adaptations can be unlearned.

HOW TO BEGIN HEALING YOUR PATTERNS

It is very important to understand that healing does not mean becoming a different person. Though the process can lead to a different expression or version of who you are. But healing does involve becoming a person who includes your*self* in the circle of care. And this is a wonderful thing!

Here's how that begins.

1. Name (Identify) the Pattern Without Shame

Shame keeps patterns alive. Naming them brings them into the light so you can release them.

You can say:

- "I over-function when I'm overwhelmed."
- "I silence myself to keep the peace (but realize this is self-abandonment)."
- "I take responsibility for things that aren't mine."
- "I feel guilty for resting."

Naming is identifying the pattern. It is the first step toward change.

2. Practice Micro-Boundaries

Small, consistent micro boundaries of help in establishing balance are more effective than big huge ones. They set a pace that is non-threatening and eases into change. However, there will be moments when a more drastic measure or boundary is necessary. It is important to adapt and be prepared for either. When not in full crisis mode, the micro boundaries are very effective and often prevent or discourage feeding into the chaos or trauma. Therefore, helping to redirect it away. This is also very helpful in reducing patterns. Remember that old adage, the tortoise finished the race before the hare? Micro boundaries in essence are the tortoise. Grounded, slow, deliberate.

Examples:

- "I need a minute."
- "I can help after I rest."
- "I can do one thing, not three."
- "I'm not available right now."

Micro-boundaries teach you that your needs matter.

3. Let Yourself Be Personal

You are allowed to:

- be tired
- be frustrated
- be overwhelmed
- need help
- make mistakes
- take breaks
- have limits

You are someone carrying a heavy load. It is recommended to pause and reclaim your moment.

4. Reclaim One Small Piece of Yourself

Choose one thing that belongs to you:

- a hobby
- a ritual
- a walk
- a book
- a moment of silence
- a creative practice

Reclaiming even one small piece of yourself begins the process of rebuilding your identity.

5. Challenge the Guilt Gently

When guilt arises, ask:

- "Is this guilt or exhaustion?"
- "Is this guilt or conditioning?"
- "Is this guilt or fear?"

Most caregiver guilt is misplaced so identifying it reduces its attachment.

6. Allow Yourself to Receive Support

Receiving support is part of regulation. The result of this most often is growth!

Support can look like:

- asking a friend to sit with you
- accepting help with meals
- letting someone else handle a task
- joining a caregiver group
- talking to a therapist
- taking respite care

Remember that caregivers don't have to carry everything alone. Knowing when to reach outward is really an action of growth. And growth expands.

7. Repair With Yourself in Mind

Just as you repair with others, you must repair with yourself.

You can acknowledge when:

- "You pushed yourself too hard."
- "You deserve rest."
- "You are learning to take care of you."
- "You won't abandon you again."

Self-repair is in part self-regulation.

THE TRUTH ABOUT HEALING

Healing your patterns is really about becoming present. Living and experiencing in the moment and manifesting from that moment. This requires being present.

It's about learning to:

- pause
- breathe
- choose differently
- include yourself
- soften your expectations
- honor your limits
- trust your needs

Healing is definitely more of a relationship with yourself than an end result. So, allow the journey to create the new fond acceptance. Allow it to shape into something expansive. And allow enjoyment of the process as well. Joy won't let you down. It will help you accept happiness.

The next chapter is aimed for you to do something many caregivers struggle with:

Asking for help without guilt.

CHAPTER 13
ASKING FOR HELP

Caregivers' strengths can be resilience, patience and compassion. As well as empathy, discipline and loyalty. It is no wonder they can be the strongest people in the room.

They step in and anticipate needs, hold the emotional climate together and stay steady when others fall apart. They keep going long after their body whispers "enough."

But strength becomes a burden when it turns into isolation. And isolation is painful. It is really a human suffering.

This chapter will explore why asking for help feels impossible for so many strong givers. Showing why it's not your fault, and how to begin opening the door to support without guilt, shame, or fear.

WHY ASKING FOR HELP FEELS SO HARD

Most caregivers struggle with asking for help because of learned behaviour; a misguided code that they created stating self-reliance equals safety. It can feel really foreign and uncomfortable.

Here are the most common reasons asking for help feels impossible:

1. You Learned Early That You Had to Be the Strong One

Many caregivers grew up in environments where:

- adults were unavailable
- emotions were unpredictable
- responsibilities fell on them
- they had to mature quickly
- they learned to survive by being capable

Your nervous system learned:
"If I don't do it, no one will."

This belief becomes a lifelong pattern.

2. You Don't Want to Burden Anyone

Caregivers often say:

- "Everyone else has their own problems."
- "I don't want to be a bother."
- "I don't want to inconvenience anyone."

But this belief usually comes from a deeper truth:

You were taught that your needs were too much. Or exaggerated.

So, you learned to shrink them! Come on caregivers – we do this all the time!

3. You Feel Guilty for Needing Anything

Guilt is one of the heaviest emotions caregivers carry.

Guilt for:

- resting
- asking for help
- wanting time alone

- feeling overwhelmed
- not being perfect
- being human
- being reactive

But guilt is actually a trauma response.

4. You're Afraid Things Will Fall Apart Without You

Caregivers often believe:

- "No one else can do it right."
- "It's easier to do it myself."
- "If I step away, everything will collapse."

This is hypervigilance. It is anything but arrogance. It is a genuine fear something harmful can happen.

Your nervous system has been in charge for so long that letting go feels dangerous. This danger is not towards themselves; they are afraid for the person they are caring for.

5. You Don't Trust That Help Will Actually Help

Many caregivers have been disappointed before:

- people who offered help but didn't follow through
- people who minimized the situation
- people who made things harder
- people who judged instead of supported
- people who felt obligated they were asked for help

Your nervous system remembers these experiences and the memory it has so deeply ingrained, it protects you by avoiding more of them.

THE COST OF DOING EVERYTHING ALONE

Doing everything alone feels safer, until it doesn't.

The cost is high:

- burnout
- resentment
- exhaustion
- health issues
- emotional numbness
- loss of identity
- chronic stress
- isolation

You cannot sustain caregiving without support. No one can. Asking for help is necessary.

HOW TO BEGIN ASKING FOR HELP (WITHOUT GUILT)

You can start with small, gentle steps. Regulate the timing and the process. Let it be a journey.

1. Start With Micro-Asks

Micro-asks are small, low-risk requests that help your nervous system practice receiving support.

Examples:

- "Can you pick up milk on your way home?"
- "Can you sit with them for 10 minutes while I shower?"
- "Can you help me carry this?"

Micro-asks build trust in others and in yourself.

2. Ask for Specific, Concrete Help

People want to help, but they don't know how.

When someone asks:

"Let me know if you need anything."

Try:

"I could use help with dinner on Tuesday."
"Could you stay with her for an hour this weekend?"
"Could you call me once a week to check in?"

Specificity reduces overwhelm for everyone. And when you define your needs, you also understand them within yourself. And can organize better.

3. Let People Do Things Imperfectly

Support won't always look the way you would do it. That's okay. Letting go of perfection is part of healing.

You can say: "It doesn't have to be perfect; I just need the help."

Your nervous system will resist this at first. That's normal.

4. Build a Support Circle, not a Single Lifeline

No one person can meet all your needs. You need a network. Not one single life-line.

Your support circle might include:

- family
- friends
- neighbors
- respite care
- support groups
- community programs
- therapists
- volunteers

Support is a mosaic, not a single tile.

5. Practice Receiving Without Apologizing

When someone helps you, resist the urge to say:

- "I'm sorry."
- "I hate to ask."
- "I feel bad."

Instead, try:

"Thank you, this means a lot."
"I appreciate your help."

Receiving is a skill. The bonus to this is, it gets easier with practice.

6. Challenge the Belief That You Must Earn Rest

You don't have to be exhausted or falling apart to deserve support. You can take it before that time arrives. And remember, you don't have to justify your needs.

You deserve rest because it is healthy and balanced. Not because you've reached your breaking point. It is better not to wait until that point.

7. Let Your Nervous System Learn That Help Is Safe

At first, asking for help will feel uncomfortable. It could make your body tense, your mind may resist and as a result, your guilt may flare.

This is a sign that you're doing something new that requires a different action that will create a difference response. Your sub-conscious wants to keep you safe so it wants to recreate the same response and keep you feeling guilty. Resist this urge.

Your nervous system needs time to learn that:

- help is safe
- support is allowed
- you don't have to carry everything
- you are not alone

This learning is very healing so give it time! It is really worth to be patient with the steps towards it and the results that derive from something as simple as rest.

THE TRUTH ABOUT ASKING FOR HELP

Asking for help is a wisdom. It's letting people in by allowing connection.

It's sharing the load. You don't have to do everything alone and you won't lose control when you allow this.

For those caregivers that have tried to ask for help, but instead, got a slammed door, or a silence instead of yes, please try again.

I am sorry for the rejection you have experienced at a time you really needed care. I don't have the answers to why that happened, but please do not allow yourself to stop or feel it was because you were not worthy. It was more about what the other person couldn't do than if you were worth it.

I pray that you trust the lessons and advice in this book to try again. It will be worth it. You will see. Keep expanding.

SECTION V - Moving Forward Together

CHAPTER 14

REPAIRING FAMILY RELATIONSHIPS AFTER CHAOS

Chaos leaves marks. It often can be very destructive to the family fabric. It isn't because families don't love each other but because nerves under pressure make you say and do things the heart never intended to express.

Caregiving, dementia, PTSD, anxiety, trauma, these states strain relationships in ways most people can't understand. But those that have lived them understand all too well how devastating the outcome can be. Words get sharper. Patience gets thinner. Misunderstandings multiply. People withdraw. People explode. People shut down. People disconnect.

And afterward, when the storm passes, families are left with the quiet or enormous ache of:

- "I didn't mean that."
- "I wish I could take it back."
- "I don't know how to fix this."
- "I feel so far away from them."
- "We used to be closer."

Repair is how families find their way back to each other. This is the aim.

Repair is about reconnecting with a recognition of what happened, not a blind eye that nothing happened. Chaos is there and can not be ignored

This chapter teaches you how to rebuild safety, trust, and connection. Thoughtfully, slowly, and without shame.

WHY REPAIR MATTERS

Repair is the antidote to rupture.

Rupture happens when:

- someone yells
- someone shuts down
- someone withdraws
- someone forgets
- someone reacts
- someone gets overwhelmed
- someone says something they regret
- someone ghosts
- someone walks away

Rupture is inevitable in traumata infused families. Repair is what keeps the relationship alive.

Repair teaches the nervous system:

- conflict is survivable
- connection can return
- safety can be rebuilt
- love is still present
- loyalty is deserved

Without repair, families drift but with repair, families heal.

THE FOUNDATIONS OF REPAIR

1. Repair Begins with Regulation, Not Words

You cannot repair from a dysregulated state or still activate in that state.

Before repair, you need:

- a pause
- a breath
- a moment of grounding
- space to settle
- time to soften
- time to understand and evaluate, discern

Repair requires a regulated body, not a perfect script.

2. Repair Is About Connection, Not Correction

Repair does not require:

- explaining
- defending
- justifying
- proving a point
- revisiting the argument

Repair is:

- acknowledging
- validating
- reconnecting
- softening
- rebuilding trust

A key note here is that you're not trying to win instead, see it as trying to return to each other.

3. Repair Must Be Simple

In trauma, long conversations overwhelm the nervous system; the brain.

Repair works best when it's short and simple.

Examples:

- "I'm sorry for how I reacted."
- "I didn't mean to hurt you."
- "That was a hard moment."
- "I was really hurting. I didn't mean to lash out"
- "I care about you."
- "We're okay."

Simple words carry deep healing.

HOW TO REPAIR AFTER CHAOS

Step 1: Acknowledge the Moment

Remember identifying the moment creates the awareness. Analyzing can wait.

Examples:

- "That was a tough moment."
- "Things got intense earlier."
- "We both felt overwhelmed."

identifying reduces shame and opens the door to connection.

Step 2: Take Responsibility for Your Part (Not Theirs)

Responsibility is ownership, maturity and opposite of blame.

Examples:

- "I'm sorry for my tone."
- "I reacted too quickly."
- "I shut down and I didn't mean to."

You're not taking responsibility for the entire moment, just your piece.

This creates safety. And truth that builds trust and repair.

Step 3: Validate Their Experience

Validation soothes the entire nervous system. It creates relief.

Examples:

- "I see why you felt upset."
- "It makes sense you were overwhelmed."
- "I understand why that was hard."

Validation is acknowledgment. It is different from agreement.

Step 4: Reconnection

Reconnection can be:

- a soft tone
- a hand on the shoulder
- sitting together

- a shared activity
- a warm drink
- a quiet moment

Connection doesn't always require words.

Step 5: Create a Small Plan for Next Time

It does not have to be a big plan, or a perfect plan. I recommend a small one.

Examples:

- "Next time, let's pause sooner."
- "Let's use our calm phrase."
- "Let's take a break before it escalates."

Small plans create predictability. Predictability creates safety.

REPAIR IN DEMENTIA, PTSD, AND ANXIETY

Repair looks different depending on the condition.

Repair in Dementia

Dementia affects memory, but emotionally, events are alive.

Even if they forget the argument, an emotional residue remains.

Repair can be:

- a gentle tone

- a soft touch
- a calm presence
- a simple reassurance: “We’re okay.”
- When appropriate- a hug.

Emotional repair matters more than verbal repair.

Repair in PTSD

PTSD makes people feel unsafe after conflict.

Repair must be:

- slow
- gentle
- predictable
- non-threatening

Examples:

- “We’re safe.”
- “I’m here.”
- “We can slow down.”
- “I understand.”

Safety is the foundation.

Repair in Anxiety

Anxiety magnifies misunderstandings.

Repair must be:

- clear

- steady
- reassuring

Examples:

- "It will be okay."
- "We'll figure this out."
- "I'm not upset with you."

Clarity calms the anxious mind.

WHEN REPAIR ISN'T IMMEDIATE

Sometimes repair can't happen right away.

That's okay.

You can say:

- "I need a little time, but I care about you."
- "Let's come back to this later, I do want to talk about it."
- "I'm not ready yet, but I'm not going anywhere."

Delayed repair is still repair. Be patient with the process, yourself and the outcome.

THE TRUTH ABOUT REPAIR

Repair is about return.

It's about saying:

- “We’re still connected.”
- “We can get through this.”
- “We’re on the same team.”
- “We can try again.”

Repair is how families heal, bit by bit.

CHAPTER 15

FINDING MOMENTS OF JOY AGAIN

When a family has lived in survival mode for a long time, joy can feel foreign, even suspicious.

You get so used to:

- bracing
- anticipating
- managing
- calming
- fixing
- absorbing
- enduring
- ignoring

... that joy becomes something you don't trust anymore.

You may even feel guilty when joy appears, as if you're not allowed to feel good while someone you love is struggling. Or as if joy is a luxury reserved for people with easier lives.

But joy is not a luxury. Joy is a form of resilience. It is a medicine worth taking and it is essential to living. This chapter will help you rediscover joy, not as a forced positivity, or denial, but as a gentle return to the parts of life that make you feel alive again. I truly believe joy is necessary for hope.

WHY JOY FEELS HARD AFTER LONG PERIODS OF STRESS

1. You have Been in Survival Mode

When the body is in fight, flight, or freeze, it cannot access joy because your prioritizing survival. It has little to do with wanting it or not.

Joy requires:

- safety
- presence
- openness
- capacity

Survival mode shuts all of that down.

2. You've Learned to Expect the Next Crisis

Caregivers often say:

- "Every time things feel calm, something happens."
- "I can't relax; it never lasts."
- "I'm always waiting for the next problem."
- "It will be taken away somehow."

This anticipation steals joy before it can land.

3. You Feel Guilty Experiencing Joy When Others Are Suffering

This guilt is common. You may think:

- "How can I enjoy myself when they're struggling?"
- "It feels selfish to take a break."

- "I shouldn't be happy when things are so hard."

Joy replenishes you so you can keep going. So, remember, your joy will not take anything away from a family member. It will fortify you and in turn fortify them. It will give you hope for the future and light the path for them.

4. You've Forgotten What Joy Feels Like

When you've been overwhelmed for a long time, joy becomes unfamiliar.
It feels distant and unreachable. It feels like something that belongs to another version of you.

Joy at this stage is buried or dormant, not lost forever. It can and will return.

THE TRUTH ABOUT JOY WHEN THERE IS TRAUMA

Joy more than not will return in spurts; in moments; not all at once.

These moments are small, quiet ones. Even unexpected ones. Joy is the presence of something good *despite* the stress.

Joy can also require practice.

HOW TO REDISCOVER JOY (SLOWLY)

1. Start With Micro-Joy

Micro-joy is tiny, fleeting, sensory joy.

Examples:

- warm sunlight on your face
- a favorite song
- a quiet cup of tea
- a soft blanket
- a moment of laughter
- a deep breath that actually feels good
- a flower on your walk
- a memory that warms you
- your pet brushing against you

Micro-joy is small enough for a tired nervous system to receive.

2. Let Joy Be Simple

You need small joys that fit into your daily life.

Joy can be:

- sitting outside for two minutes
- watching a bird
- smelling something comforting
- listening to a calming sound
- noticing something beautiful

Simple joy is sustainable joy.

3. Allow Joy Without Earning It

You don't have to:

- finish all your tasks
- solve all the problems
- be fully rested
- be perfectly regulated
- have a peaceful home

... to deserve joy.

Joy is not a reward; it is a state of being and deserved.

4. Let Joy Coexist with Hardship

Joy and pain can exist in the same moment.

You can be exhausted and still laugh.
You can be grieving and still feel warmth.
You can be overwhelmed and still experience beauty.

Joy does not erase hardship but it can soften it.

5. Create Tiny Rituals of Pleasure

Rituals anchor joy into your day.

Examples:

- lighting a candle in the evening
- a morning stretch
- a favorite mug
- a short walk

- a song that lifts you
- a nightly moment of gratitude
- a weekly treat

Rituals give your nerves something to look forward to.

6. Let Connection Be a Source of Joy

Connection doesn't have to be deep or long.
It can be:

- a shared smile
- a gentle touch
- a moment of eye contact
- a small joke
- a quiet moment sitting together

Connection is one of the most powerful forms of joy.

7. Notice Joy When It Happens

Joy often appears quietly.

When you notice it, see it and claim it:

- "This feels good."
- "This moment matters."
- "I want to remember this."

Claiming joy helps your nervous system register it and hold it.

JOY AS A FORM OF RESILIENCE

Joy is:

- nerves in repair
- emotional nourishment
- a return to yourself
- a reminder that life is more than survival
- a way to stay human in the middle of hardship

Joy gives you the strength to face hardship. The hope to get through it and that, it will pass.

CHAPTER 16

BUILDING A FUTURE THAT FEELS POSSIBLE

When you've lived in survival mode for a long time, the future can feel like a threat instead of a promise. You stop imagining. You stop dreaming. You stop planning. You stop hoping. You freeze. You go on hold.

This can feel vacant and bleak. Your central nervous system has learned that unpredictability equals danger so it stopped believing.

Caregiving, trauma, dementia, PTSD, anxiety... these experiences shrink your sense of what's possible. They make you focus on the next hour, the next task, the next behavior, the next crisis. Long-term thinking becomes exhaustive. And you don't even try to plan.

But you deserve a future that feels possible. A future you can co-create and manifest. And shape to your desires.

This chapter helps you gently expand your sense of what tomorrow can hold, without overwhelming you or ignoring the realities of your life. So, you don't feel so lost and directionless.

WHY THE FUTURE FEELS SCARY AFTER LONG PERIODS OF STRESS

1. Your Nervous System Has Been Trained to Expect Crisis

When you've lived in a state of constant alertness, your body assumes the future will be more of the same.

This makes planning feel:

- pointless
- overwhelming
- unsafe
- unrealistic
- scary

You're protecting yourself from disappointment or even more than that, safety or harm.

2. You've Been Operating Without Capacity

When you're exhausted, burned out, or emotionally depleted, the future feels too big to think about.

You may feel:

- "I can barely get through today."
- "I don't have the energy to plan anything."
- "I don't know what I want anymore."
- I thought I could do this, but it feels too big."

This is not a lack of ambition or being lazy. It is truly a lack of physical, mental and emotional capacity.

3. You've Lost Touch with Your Own Needs and Desires

Caregiving often consumes your identity.

You may not know:

- what you enjoy
- what you want
- what you need
- what you dream about
- what makes you feel alive

4. You're Afraid to Hope

Hope feels dangerous when life has been this way.

You may think:

- "If I hope, I'll get hurt."
- "If I plan, something will go wrong."
- "If I look forward to something, it won't happen."

  Or

I don't know how to hope, what does that feel like? What does that entail? I can't remember what that feels like anymore. I only know this current state of: numbness, heaviness, exhaustion.

This is trauma speaking, not truth.

THE FUTURE DOESN'T HAVE TO BE BIG - IT JUST HAS TO BE YOURS

You need a future that feels:

- gentle
- possible

- grounded
- flexible
- compassionate
- real
- yours

A future that honours you neurologically, your limits, and your spirit. Put aside the vision board or 5year plan for now. Start with a micro-plan.

HOW TO BUILD A FUTURE THAT FEELS POSSIBLE

1. Start With Micro-Futures

A micro-future is a small, manageable thing you can look forward to. As mentioned in previous chapters there can be many micros. Here it is steps that can be your micro-future.

Examples:

- a quiet morning
- a walk tomorrow
- a favorite meal
- a phone call with someone you trust
- a moment of rest
- a small ritual you enjoy

Micro-futures rebuild your capacity for hope.

2. Create Gentle, Flexible Plans

Rigid plans are known to overwhelm while simple plans support.

Examples:

- "Sometime this week, I want to read for 10 minutes."
- "This month, I want one afternoon to myself."
- "This season, I want to reconnect with someone I love."

Flexibility reduces pressure and increases possibility.

3. Reclaim One Small Dream

Just one small dream that belongs to you.

Maybe:

- learning something new
- returning to a hobby
- writing again
- gardening
- traveling locally
- creating something
- reconnecting with a part of yourself

Small dreams rebuild identity.

4. Build a Future That Includes Support

A sustainable future is one where you are not carrying everything alone.

This might include:

- respite care
- shared responsibilities
- community programs
- support groups
- therapy
- family involvement

- hired help when possible

Support is your infrastructure.

5. Let Your Future Be Imperfect

Your future doesn't have to be:

- tidy
- predictable
- linear
- impressive
- Instagram-worthy

It just has to be yours.

6. Allow Yourself to Want Things Again

Desire is a sign of healing.

You are allowed to want:

- rest
- joy
- connection
- time
- space
- creativity
- pleasure
- ease

Wanting is the beginning of your self-expression and reconnection

7. Build a Future with Room for You

Your future cannot be built entirely around caregiving.

You need:

- your own rituals
- your own relationships
- your own identity
- your own dreams
- your own rest
- your own life

You matter too.

THE TRUTH ABOUT MOVING FORWARD

Moving forward doesn't mean:

- forgetting the past
- pretending things are easy
- ignoring the hard parts
- abandoning the people you care for

Moving forward means:

- expanding your capacity
- reclaiming your identity
- allowing hope
- building support
- creating space for yourself
- **imagining possibilities again**

Remember: your future just has to be possible.

CHAPTER 17

CELEBRATE YOUR COURAGE, YOUR HEART AND YOUR CARE

If you've made it to this chapter, it means you've lived through things most people won't. You have carried responsibilities that were incredibly heavy, on the brink of absurd. You've held emotions that were enormous.

You've survived days that felt impossible.

And you're still here. I applaud you.

This final chapter is not about tools or strategies but simply put:
It all about honouring you. So, celebrate.

THE TRUTH ABOUT YOUR JOURNEY

Caregiving, trauma, dementia, PTSD and anxiety are experiences that reshape a person. They change how you see yourself, how you act or face the world, how you relate to others, and how you understand yourself. They can often be permanent changes to your personality or your lifestyle, because you cannot unsee or unhear your experiences.

You may have felt:

- invisible
- overwhelmed
- misunderstood

- unappreciated
- isolated
- exhausted
- afraid
- numb
- responsible for everything
- unlovable
- rejected

You may have questioned:

- "Am I doing enough?"
- "Why is this so hard?"
- "What's wrong with me?"
- "Why can't I handle this better?"
- "Will things ever get easier?"
- "Why am I so misunderstood?"
- "Why doesn't anyone care."
- "Why is this all on my shoulders? Hello?"

You've been carrying a lot; it is okay to just acknowledge it is a lot.

YOU DO NOT HAVE TO DO THIS ALONE ANYMORE

The world often tells caregivers:

- "You're so strong."
- "You're amazing."
- "I don't know how you do it."

But what you really needed was:

- "How can I support you?"

- "You deserve rest."
- "You don't have to do this alone."
- "Your needs matter too."
- "Please, let me help."

The starkest fact is you were never meant to isolate and survive. But somehow, life got complicated and you just did.

THE POWER OF BEING SEEN – Get your voice heard

You deserve to be seen, not just for what you do, but for who you are.

You deserve to be recognized for:

- your patience
- your resilience
- your tenderness
- your endurance
- your adaptability
- your courage
- your humanity

You deserve to be acknowledged for the invisible labour you carry every day, supported for it not just given a pat on the back.

THE FUTURE IS NOT SOMETHING YOU HAVE TO FEAR

Your future doesn't have to be defined by crisis or by overwhelm. And it no longer has to be built on self-sacrifice.

Your future can be:

- simpler

- slower
- more supported
- more connected
- more spacious
- more yours

Be patient at this juncture because you may not know what your future looks like. It may be a blank page. And blank pages can be scary. Let this time settle. You don't have to know exactly what it looks like either. You only have to accept you're allowed.

YOU ARE WORTHY OF CARE

You deserve all these things:

- rest
- support
- joy
- connection
- understanding
- compassion
- boundaries
- healing

Even when it feels like no one understands; when the nights are long or the days heavy.
And it feels like tomorrow never comes. You will get through this, and remember, that you have support.

I am sorry you have had moments, months even years when you have felt alone. These moments were long and drawn out. They were isolating and bleak. But please know this:

There are others walking this path with you, who understand this kind of exhaustion. Others navigating the same storms; feeling the same aches.

Support is here; support that is tangible, seen and felt. You are allowed to rest, to receive and be cared for too.

I want this book to be part of your beginning, a moment to end the day that never came. This is my hope. This is the brand-new day that has arrived. It is yours so claim it. Hold on to it. Never let it go. Why? Because you matter, and change matters.

You've named your nerves, your patterns, your limits, your needs, and your worth.

You are here, in a space you have connected and created simply by devoting a little time to yourself.

PART II

RETURNING

INTRODUCTION

I never expected that the very teachings I offered in Part I would become the lifeline I needed next. I wrote WHEN CARING HURTS as a guide, a compass, a way to help others navigate the weight of caring - because I understood it, because I had lived it, and because I was still living it. But then life, in its synchronistic way, asked me to embody every word in real time.

It shouldn't surprise me, and yet it does. It feels like art merging with reality, truth bleeding forward into the future. How incredibly potent. And if anyone ever dares to question or diminish this work, I will remember this exact juncture - right here, right now - and remind them that I am living proof.

This is the moment my story shifts - where the coach becomes the student, and the woman behind the wisdom steps forward open and human. People often ask me, *Who coaches the coach when you're the one in need?* My answer has always been the same: life itself, and the good people around me who care enough to listen and love back.

If Part I was the lantern I held out for others, Part II is the moment I realized I needed light myself. Everything I had taught, everything I had poured into coaching, suddenly became the very tools I had to use to walk through my own challenge. It is one thing to teach these principles; it is another to live them and rise through them. That is what defines you.

This is why I am so determined in my coaching and so boldly honest. Many of my clients call it "brutally honest," but the truth is simpler: I don't want anyone to give up or walk through unnecessary suffering. I want to spare them the pain I've known. But I also understand that people move through life in their own way, on their own timeline.

Watching from the sidelines can be bitterly painful when you carry someone in your heart. With family, that ache cuts even deeper. The pain comes from knowing what could change if they stopped long enough to listen - and knowing they may choose not to. Loving deeply makes that knowledge gut-wrenching.

Part II is me, right now, living the truth of what I teach. This is where my heart speaks without performance. This is where the journey becomes real - sending shivers down my spine, tears down my cheek, and a quiet sigh of relief, because I know this too will pass.

CHAPTER ONE

THE BODY'S TELL-TELL

Anticipation of pain; the snap!

I knew it was coming before it happened but chose to plod along anyway. Not even thinking of the aftermath. It was sudden and felt strange, a sort of electric impulse ignited within me. My body tightened a split second before it was about to collapse. It was very subtle but alerting, and I did not miss the warning it gave. I watched myself became agitated while pressure began to build. A tightening in my chest signaled my brain; *Brace yourself because something is about to snap.*

For months, maybe longer, I had been living inside a lot of pressure. Ignoring it. Negotiating with it. Pretending I could outrun it if I just kept moving, giving, keeping it together with my sheer will do it. I had committed to helping, even if it came at me without choice. I wasn't acknowledging the toll it was taking on me. But one thing I have learned is that our body always keeps score. Mine had grown tired of my bargaining with it.

It started first with my pain in my ears. A sudden deep, dull ache that felt like someone was pressing their thumb into the side of my head. A pressure that built slowly, then suddenly surged, as if my body was trying to speak through the only channel I couldn't ignore. I remember touching the side of my face, half-expecting to find heat or swelling, something visible to justify the pain. But there was nothing. Just the quiet insistence of my body accepting the pain in silence. It was there but I ignored it for months and months.

Then came the moment I snapped. A moment where something inside me gave way. The rubber band stretched and tore. Right in the middle. There was no way to ignore it.

Even after persistent commitment to watch my reactions; I found ways to take responsibility for my intensity, my passion. Let's face it. I am the girl you want to arrive in a 911 call. I am all in with both feet, ready to take action, knowing what to do way before anyone else. People don't always appreciate that. Especially in arguments. I have learned to be more cerebral and less reactive. Kind of.

Back to when I snapped. It was small, almost imperceptible. But I felt it as a shift, a moment when I observed my tension hit a peak. My body had spoken, and this time, it didn't negotiate. It didn't ask for permission. It simply said, *No more.*

And in that instant, I knew I was crossing a threshold I couldn't uncross. The kind of moment that announces itself with an oddly serene, yet devastating certainty. Like the calm before the storm. Something in me had reached enough and I wasn't sure yet whether it was the breaking point or the actual beginning.

Reflection

The body speaks long before the mind is willing to listen. It warns us. It whispers, it aches, it tightens. And when we ignore it, it eventually snaps. This happens not to punish us, but to actually stop us. This was the moment mine stopped asking and started showing me, enough.

CHAPTER TWO

THE COLLAPSE

physical exhaustion, bedridden

When exhaustion is chronic, sleep can't touch it. It doesn't come from a long day or a restless night, but from years of carrying what was never meant to be carried alone. It settles into the body and finds refuge in the bones, your joints, all along your spine, your neck, your temples. It becomes a weight you stop noticing until it finally pins you down.

The morning my body caved; I woke up without the feeling of having slept at all. Instead, it felt like a truck had just hit me and actually woken me from somewhere else. Maybe a roadside. My face felt like a cement block on my pillow and the pillow itself, felt like a sack of sand.

I was in bed but I remember not being able to sleep; tossing and turning. My body heating up all night with cramping in my legs and hips. Everything felt sore.

My body felt foreign, heavy in a way that frightened me. My limbs didn't respond with their usual automatic motion of picking me up from the bed. Even lifting my head felt like trying to move through water. I remember staring at the ceiling, realizing with a kind of stunned clarity that I couldn't get up. Not that I didn't want to, or that I needed a minute. I just couldn't. My body said no.

I tried to negotiate with it, the old habit. Maybe it wasn't really negotiating. It was me just pushing with all my might to get up. But nothing moved. Not even the smallest nudge.

It was as if my body had finally staged a coup. And this was really frightening.

The pressure in my ears pulsed a rhythmic reminder that something inside me had been straining. My chest felt tight from depletion. Everything started to feel numb. And a kind of blankness came over me.

I lay there, staring at the ceiling, immobilized; realizing that this wasn't fatigue. This was a collapse.

It just arrived. Even after all those ignored signs. My body had been signaling for many months and I ignored every plea it made for me to slow down and rest.

I wasn't just tired. I was done not listening.

And in that stillness that forced an unmoving surrender; something inside me finally admitted the truth: I had crossed a line I didn't even know I was approaching. A line between functioning and dying. Between coping and breaking.

I wasn't the caregiver in that moment. I wasn't anything but a body that had reached its limit.

And for the first time in a very long time, I had no choice but to listen.

Reflection

Collapse isn't a weakness. It's the body's last act of protection. When you've pushed past every warning sign, something steps in and shuts itself down in a last attempt to save what's left. This was the moment my body refused to let me continue disappearing into care.

CHAPTER THREE

THE MELTING POINT

tears, release, the crack in the armour

This is the moment the tears finally came through. You cannot blink them away, or swallow them down with a deep breath. There comes a time when they just pour out of you like the tip of Niagara Falls; gushing towards you with all the force nature has to deliver.

My tears arrived without warning. For the longest time, I had stopped crying. I remember the moment when the accumulation of all the years of pain came to a point and a little voice inside my head said: No more tears. This of course, bothered me deeply but I had no choice. It was triggered and that was that. The tears stopped. But the morning of my collapse, the tears unblocked.

I was still in bed, still pinned by exhaustion, when the first tear slipped down the side of my face. It startled me. I hadn't cried in so long that I'd almost forgotten what it felt like. I'd become an expert at holding myself together, at swallowing my hurts. Not always polished, but none the less, I grew an armour. I don't even know why I had become that way. I can only remember the pain had cut so deep; and it happened so often, I had grown so tired of crying, that I think all my tears dried up! And my heart grew a shield. All on its own. Without my choosing it. I had always disliked it when people didn't show true emotion or true hurt. In opposite to strength, I felt not showing emotion was weak.

That morning, my numbness awoke.

It was a warm tear; the kind that feels like recognition from the soul. One tear became two, then three, and then suddenly I was crying in a way I hadn't cried in years. Not from sadness alone, but from the sheer weight of everything I had buried deep within me and all I had carried without pause.

The tears became hot, insistent and I could feel the swelling of my heart. They carried months of swallowed frustration, years of unspoken grief, and the silent ache of being the responsible one while slowly unraveling inside.

I cried from the sheer exhaustion. I cried because of the pressure and the incredible unfairness. All the responsibility rested on my shoulders. I cried for that part of me that kept pushing long after she should have stopped. I cried because my body had finally forced me to feel what my mind had avoided.

But I also cried because my heart was breaking from the pain, I knew my loved ones felt too. And I couldn't make them feel better. The pain they felt would be there as it had been for years.

And as the tears kept coming, something inside me shifted. There was a melting point.

The moment the frozen parts of me thawed just enough to let the truth rise. The moment I realized I wasn't breaking down; I was breaking open.

The crying relieved my worry I would never feel again. It didn't solve the exhaustion or erase the years of strain, but it proved I was still capable of feeling. Reminding me I was still alive. And that I hadn't grown cold, bitter or turned to stone. I was so relieved. I hadn't reached that point, that it was only a fear.

And in that perfectly raw, trembling moment, I understood something I had forgotten: tears are the body's way of releasing what the heart can no longer carry alone.

Reflection

The melting point is the moment the armour or numbness gives way because you finally reach the truth. Tears are the body's permission to feel again. They mark the shift from surviving to awakening, from holding everything in to letting go and expressing again, emoting, being awake and present in the here and now. Even if the here and now means experiencing the truth of pain, exhaustion and change. Knowing the hardline is drawn.

CHAPTER FOUR

THE MOMENT OF TRUTH

the thing you can't not feel

After I cried, silence followed. It was a settling silence. It felt like dust drifting through a sunbeam after something inside fell apart into many little pieces. I sat in the silence; my face damp, my breath uneven, my body still too heavy to move. And in that stillness, I understood there was no conclusion.

But a feeling arose that was a deep, resonant knowing as it spread through my chest like warmth after a long freeze. It was the kind of truth that doesn't ask to be understood. It simply *is*. And once it appears, you can't not feel it.

The truth was that I had been disappearing. I had become invisible to myself, to my family and to the rest of my community. I was slowly but steadily disappearing.

Slowly, quietly, in the way caregivers do; piece by piece, need by need, crisis by crisis. I had been giving myself away in small, almost invisible increments, until there was barely anything left to hold.

And my body, loyal and patient as it had been, finally refused to let me continue.

I realized then that the collapse was the pause I needed. It was a boundary. A line drawn by the part of me that still wanted to live.

The pressure, the unbearable pain in my back, in my hips and legs, the exhaustion, the tears; these weren't random symptoms. They were messages. They were my way of saying; *you cannot keep going like this. You cannot keep abandoning yourself. You must stop.*

It was a truth I had avoided for years because acknowledging it would mean something had to change. And change, for a caregiver, often feels like betrayal of duty, of family, of the role you've been conditioned to inhabit. It is heartbreaking.

But lying there, unable to move, stripped me of all pretense. I felt the truth settle with a clarity that was almost merciful.

I wasn't meant to carry this alone. But I had. I survived every day forgetting who I was and shifting to auto-pilot for those I loved. And the cost of pretending otherwise had finally come due.

It wasn't a dramatic revelation. It was quiet, steady and undeniable.

And once I felt it, I knew: Nothing could go back to the way it was.

Reflection

The moment of truth can arrive in the quiet after the collapse, when the body has finally expressed what the mind refused to hear. It is the knowing that cannot be unfelt, the clarity that marks the beginning of change, even before you're ready to take the first step.

CHAPTER FIVE

THE HEART OF THE MATTER

feeling again

After experiencing a collapse of this kind, there is an uncomfortable awkwardness: the world feels both too sharp and too dull at the same time. It is as if every sensation has been turned up a notch, but your body hasn't quite caught up to the fact that it is safe.

My body felt safe enough to feel again.

It started subtly. A warmth in my chest. A heaviness behind my ribs. A flicker of something I couldn't name at first, just presence. A sense of myself I hadn't felt in a long time. I could feel myself, sitting and there I was. Me with me. In a moment, a very quick moment I felt whole again.

For months, maybe years, I had been moving through life like a silhouette. Unfortunately, an ever-expanding silhouette. Doing what needed to be done. Responding. Managing. Holding. But no longer really connecting to my deeper feelings. I had become efficient at functioning without inhabiting myself. It was survival, but it was my slow disappearance.

In the quiet after the tears, something shifted. I felt my own heartbeat. Literally. A slow, steady thump against my ribs, as if my body was reminding me, *You're still here. You're still alive. You still belong to yourself.*

It was disorienting at first. Feeling again meant I had to face everything I had avoided; all the grief, the resentment, the longing, the exhaustion. It also meant I had access to something I had forgotten: my own heart.

When the heart wakes, it does wakes up truthfully. The heart is always honest. It is the mind that choses to overlook honesty.

And as I woke, I felt the ache of everything I had endured. I felt the tenderness of everything I had lost. I felt the quiet truth that I had been living on emotional autopilot to survive the drastic changes that had been imposed on my life. I also knew that I would soon after this moment, possibly go back to autopilot again. I knew that the change I needed in order to not go into autopilot meant completely walking away from my loved ones I was caring for. And I knew, in the next months ahead, that would be impossible to do. I couldn't just walk away because it would be devastating for them. This weighed on me. I felt panic for a bit but I stopped. I soon realized I could take a break and return. It didn't have to be final or extreme. I chose to take a few days completely for myself, to could heal the physical exhaustion.

Beneath all of that panic, I felt something else, something small but unmistakable.

I felt hope.

It was a sudden moment when I realized I could get back to caregiving. It didn't soar out of me, or leap but it structured my mind. I decided to give hope to my mom and sister as well. I called them to let them know, I needed a few days and that I would see them once I felt better. I talked to my sister and asked her to hold things until I could get there.

It was a small flicker like a candle in a dark room, steady and persistent.

It was the hope that comes from finally feeling again, even if what you feel is painful. I was feeling so distant from everyone, everything. Feeling again even if it pain, means you're alive. It means you haven't gone numb forever. It means there is still something inside you worth saving.

And in that moment, there with my heartbeat echoing through my chest, I realized something simple and devastating: My heart had been waiting for me to come back home. And when it felt safe, it spoke.

Reflection

When numbness lifts, it doesn't feel like triumph. It feels like truth. Feeling again, even when it hurts, is the first sign of returning to yourself. The heart wakes slowly, honestly, and without apology. And when it does, it reminds you that you are still alive, and still capable of coming home to yourself.

CHAPTER SIX

THE EMOTIONAL FLOOD

grief, anger, relief

Now that my heart had spoken, awoken and unexpectedly expressed; I didn't know what to do next.

When the heart wakes up, it doesn't always wait for the right moment. it doesn't ease you in gently or ask if you're ready. It simply opens and everything you've been holding back comes rushing through.

The flood began slowly for me. A tightening in my throat. A heaviness behind my eyes. A pressure in my chest that felt like something trying to rise upward. I thought the tears from earlier had been the release. I didn't realize they were only the beginning.

The real flood came later.

It started with grief: deep, aching grief for everything I had carried alone. Grief for the years of being the strong one, the reliable one, the one who got things done. Grief for the parts of myself I had set aside in the name of duty. Grief for the dreams I had postponed and basically sacrificed. The boundaries I had never drawn. The exhaustion I had normalized. Grief for being put into situations where defending myself meant I had to make uncomfortable choices. Choices that went against my nature, choices that created a rush of adrenaline as a result of self-defense.

Then came the frustration.

I realized a part of me held resentment even though I normalized my lifestyle. It was the slow burn. The feeling that comes from recognizing how long I'd been ignoring myself. How many times I had put everyone else before me when I was in need of hardcore rest, attention, tender loving care. I touched on my pain. How often I had minimized it because someone else needed attention more.

It was a bit of anger too. This time it wasn't big. I had worked on the big stuff last year. Now what was left was the tinge of a reality I had found coping mechanisms for. A sort of realistic truce that brought me stability but still ebbed away at my life. My biggest challenge now was how to keep caregiving at a pace I could endure while keeping me in it too. I was beyond tired of the expectations, at the unspoken roles that had shaped my life. I held a sadness at myself for abandoning my own needs so thoroughly that my body had to intervene. This was so totally opposite of everything I had known and everything I had lived by in the past. When did this happen? When did I adopt a way of life, a coping that was against everything I believed and had trained myself to be!

At the same time of understanding my own limitations, I was also deeply saddened that both my mom and sister needed more care than I could give them. They needed more than just me. And I understood that in this moment, my wholeness was wrapped around figuring out how to get that to them.

Our situation had become much more than the system ignoring our family needs; we all needed support. I had tried getting both of them into an assisted living program. Whether in the comfort of the house or outside of it. I wanted them to understand they were at the juncture of needing help and I wanted the help to come in the home but between the system thinking we could handle it all and my family members completely refusing care – I was really stuck.

I also wanted them to choose the type of lifestyle they could transition into. But no one adapted. It was always a high-level panic and I couldn't take them feeling forced to go into care. I felt if it was pushed onto them, they wouldn't survive it. Mental illness has a breaking point. I was afraid both would not return mentally. This ebbed at my heart, my mind and my soul.

I knew where we were. My exhaustion collapse was much more than a transitory challenge; it was marking the pace of care. I wouldn't be able to do it all for them anymore. I knew the shift had come; the pace as it was, was no longer sustainable.

I begged both my mom and sister to come live with me. My mom refused. My sister, I am not sure. Sometimes I got yes, sometimes, I got "we'll see". My mom won't leave my sister alone in the house. But she doesn't like being alone there with her either. And there I was, the peace maker for the situation as I had been all my life. I was always the one stuck in the middle to solve their conundrum. Though to the outside it was as if the two of them had it all together and I was the third wheel causing upheaval, mainly because I was the vocal one. And let's be clear, I was also the reactive one. But little did anyone know how much pain being the mediator brought me. I learned from a very young age being non vocal would be my death sentence. My words were what kept me safe.

But it took a toll on me.

When a loved one is living with dementia or significant mental-health challenges, repetition becomes its own form of safety. In my mother's case, the dementia appeared suddenly. My sister, meanwhile, has carried years of mental illness. Both found stability in repeating familiar behaviours, even when those patterns offered no positive outcome. Familiarity felt safer than change.

My mother's sundowning began to escalate. At times, I would receive twenty calls within an hour. I answered most of them, knowing that any attempt to take space for myself often intensified her distress. I learned to prepare for our brief conversations, reminding her gently that I would see her soon. It was all temporary, but it was the only way to keep her anchored.

The moment I understood that my body needed rest and I would eventually return to them, a small relief settled in.

Relief that I could finally relax and possibly choose to take some time for myself. I was relieved that the numbness changed and I still had the capacity to feel. And I was relieved; I wasn't ghosting myself.

But these emotions I was feeling didn't arrive in neatly. They overlapped each other and collided. One moment I was grieving, the next I was blank again, the next I was breathing deeper as if something inside me had loosened for the first time in years.

This was the emotional cost of coming back to myself. The price of awakening after a long freeze.

My body and heart worked together to clear out everything I had stored in silence.

And as the flood moved through me, wave after wave, I realized; feeling it all was the only way through.

I saw my community and how much of my friends I lost touch with. I could feel the neglect as I walked my dog Milo through the streets. This loss hurt me deeply because my connection to everyone felt like it vanished. Literally, as I didn't run into any of my friends. And some of my neighbours moved away as well.

My collapse was the pause I needed. It was the reckoning.

And even though it left me raw and trembling, it also left me awake.

Reflection

The emotional flood usually comes with its own clarity. When the heart reawakens, it brings everything with it: the grief you buried, the frustration or anger you swallowed, the relief you didn't know you needed. Feeling it, is the only way through it. It is the beginning of healing. It is the moment you stop surviving and start returning to yourself.

CHAPTER SEVEN

THE TURNING POINT

choosing yourself

Being awake means, you have choices. Maybe because you gain understanding. Grief has loosened its grip. Frustration has untangled its cluster. Relief helped round out the edges. And in that unexpected aftermath, you start to recognize *you can't go back to the same pace b*ecause something fundamental had shifted.

I understood what I already knew, but buried; that for my own sanity and physical wellbeing, I can't disappear from myself again. I can't leap into self-preservation. The vivid reality of the morning I was framed to my bed, unable to get up appears. It was so much more final.

It was the realization that if I didn't choose myself now, I might not get another chance.

My body has drawn the boundary. My heart peaked through ever so slightly. Even as I write these next passes, a tinge of anxiety is surfacing. I can feel a small burning sensation in the left quadrant of my stomach. I don't like it. I know, it is the fear, maybe even anguish of having to get back to a pace I can't humanly endure. I have lost my roots to my home, my community and my creative freedom because my mother and sister take precedence. At the same time, I will have to sacrifice a part of my caregiving in order to heal myself. This is deadening and painful. It feels like detachment all over again. Each direction feels final.

But all turning points are final. Turning an actual page is final but it brings you to the next part of the story. I have to look at this as the next part of our story.

All that is left is the decision.

I remember reading that the body signals its limits long before an actual breakdown. In my case, the collapse came from sheer overwhelm, the cumulative weight of doing too much for too long. The signs had been there. I noticed them, questioned them, tried to respond with small pauses. But once the signals begin, even preparation only dims what's coming. The larger collapse still arrives, sometimes suddenly.

What was explained to me later is that when the body finally feels safe enough to stop bracing, it surrenders. That surrender can look like failure, but it is actually the body feeling safe enough to express what's really going on.

I couldn't quite understand why, when noticing the small triggers of overwhelm, like myself snapping, and taking a few days to regroup, my body still reacted strongly. I was confused.

But it was explained that it crashed because it felt a moment of safety to be true. Which now makes sense. I couldn't understand myself feeling good one day, then completely tightening up the next. Pushing myself through each day was just what I did. I gave it good days and bad days but I knew there was more to it. Still, my mom's and sister's needs were much more dire so I pushed along. My compassion insisted they were more important.

Now I was in the thick of what I needed too. Not just how I could keep going.

It does feel foreign at first. Self-consideration always does when you've spent years prioritizing everyone else. But I understand this is the right action, action that doesn't need justification.

Choosing myself isn't looking like a grand gesture.
It looks like letting the collapse mean something instead of rushing to

patch it over.

I am acknowledging that I was a person with limit and that those limits matter.

This is the turning point. What unsettles me is having to articulate to my mother and sister that I can no longer be present at the level I once was. I can't live there full-time anymore. I need to return to my own home at night, sleep in my own bed, and care for the family that depends on me.

For now, I also share my home with someone I regard a brother. He lives downstairs and plays a steady, essential role in caring for tmy pets and maintaining my home when I am not home. His presence is part of the structure that keeps the household functioning.

My pets: two cats and a dog have been my companions for years. Each one holds a place in my life, and when I come back to them, their welcome reminds me how much I've been away. That sense of having "abandoned" them is something I'm still working through. Emotionally it is there, a nagging pull that I miss them, and that I am somehow hurting them by being away.

What I know for certain is that splitting myself in two has taken a toll. It's created a kind of identity fracture that I can't ignore anymore.

I wake up some mornings unsure of where I am. It takes a moment before I register that I'm in my own home. Other days, I wake at my mother's house expecting to feel my dog beside me, only to remember he isn't there. And when I'm home, I still catch myself preparing to get my mother's medication before realizing I'm not with her, I'm here.

The shift has begun. I'm entering the next phase, and it will require a different kind of resilient courage.

Reflection

The turning point will happen. It's the quiet moment when you stop negotiating with your own suffering and begin to consider yourself again. Choosing yourself doesn't start with action; it starts with permission. It begins the moment you decide that your well-being is no longer optional.

CHAPTER EIGHT

THE WARMTH RETURNS

passion and clarity

Here I am. I have taken the physical space. It has been three days. There is a moment after choosing yourself whether quietly or tentatively when something inside you sparks. The pilot light relit after being blown out for so long and I am happy I felt it. My vision returned to see it as well. But I know it might go on pause again because I have to return to help my family. I really just want to take a few weeks completely to tend to my own life.

I am experiencing that instinctive, force that doesn't wait for permission. The part of me that had been buried under responsibility and exhaustion has stretched its limbs after a long coma.

Last week before all this happened, when at my mom's, I felt a sense of losing her. I was in bed and had just tucked her in, and I felt it. Losing her. It was horrible. It brought panic. But it was real. It was starting to happen. This was the change.

A change that cut through the noise and landed with certainty. I suddenly knew what I could no longer tolerate. What I could no longer carry. What I could no longer explain away. And my mom wasn't going to be happy about it. How she was going to cope was unknown. I knew I had to get resources to help but how and when was unanswered.

I had been betraying myself for years in the effort to keep my family stable. My intention was simple: I wanted them to feel safe. But the cost of that effort accumulated quietly. I love them deeply, and I know they love me. Our struggle was never about a lack of love, it was about coping. I tried to guide us toward change, offering hope without minimizing anyone's needs or dismissing the reality of what we were facing. I wanted to acknowledge all of our needs while finally learning to listen to my own.

At one point, I felt a flash of indignation, maybe, or the first spark of remembering my own worth. I had spent most of my life taking care of myself, but I had never been able to set boundaries in a way that truly protected me. I had done it in pieces, but not fully. This time, I knew I had to finish what I started. Self-respect needed to return.

I felt myself coming back, not to just cope but to co-created. To dream.

The version of me who had passions, instincts and desires that had been muted under the weight of caregiving for everyone else.

It was startling, the fire returned once I made space for it. Just for a moment. This was my dilemma. I am afraid I will stop listening because I feel my exhaustion again.

Admitting I was stuck was uncomfortable, even though I had known it for years. Ever since my mother broke her hip and my sister began reverting into a kind of rebellious adolescence, focused only on her own needs; which, given her history, was understandable, the dynamic had shifted. But they were both grown women. I was carrying my own trauma and theirs. I was the youngest, yet for so many years I had been forced into the role of the eldest. And that imbalance was never truly fair.

But this was the reality, and I accepted it. The work now was learning how to take up space again, how to speak, move, and choose a life that included me. I tried to show my mother and sister their own options as well, but each time I did, they asked me to choose for them. I wanted them to act from their own truth, yet they kept looking to me to define it.

Reflection

The fire returns quietly at first like a small flicker, a pulse, a knowing. It is the energy that stirs when you stop abandoning yourself. It brings clarity, warmth, and the courage to reclaim your place. This is not the fire of destruction, but the fire of becoming. The moment you remember who you are beneath the exhaustion.

CHAPTER NINE

THE AFTERMATH

boundaries, voice, identity and picking up the rubble

My moment of change hasn't magically fixed anything. It hasn't erased the exhaustion or undone the years of overextension I can't get back. It can't rebuild what had been worn down by caregiving, crisis, and constant vigilance. Nor the lost dreams I abandoned. And all the wrong choices.

What it has done is illuminate the landscape. I can finally see the rubble. The real, emotional debris left behind after years of pushing past my limits. The many pieces of myself I had dropped along the way. The boundaries I had set but somehow, allowed time to weaken. The voice I thought vocal but became muted. The identity I had slowly traded for responsibility.

The aftermath was one of many. But this turning point felt different. It was now or never. And I knew what never looked like. And I cried so deeply because all my life I tried to help others to not to get to this point, family included. I felt saddened for those that never took their moment, and for me now, because I knew the cost. All I could do is pray. Pray really, really deeply.

I wouldn't trade these moments of prayer for anything. I had forgotten how in the overwhelm. I had gotten so tired I didn't know how to pray anymore. I would start and then suddenly draw a blank. I couldn't hold the thought or remember the words to a prayer-or even remember what I was praying for. I was lost within myself. It felt like dementia.

I remember sitting on the edge of my bed, still tired but clearer than I had been in a long while. And for the first time, I looked at my life still with the filter of obligation but knowing I had to complete the duty to myself without the instinct to justify. Without the reflex to minimize my own needs. And this was my Achilles heal.

What I saw was stark.

I saw the patterns, the ones I had inherited, the ones I had learned, the ones I had unconsciously repeated. I saw the ways I had been conditioned to be the strong one, the reliable one, the one who absorbs everything so others don't have to.

I saw the cost of that role. Not just in my body, but in my spirit.

This aftermath wasn't about blame. And finally, it wasn't about anger. It was about truth.

The truth that I had been living in a way that was unsustainable and giving from a place of depletion. The truth that I had been disappearing inside the needs of others.

And now, I couldn't not see it.

Picking up the rubble wasn't about fixing everything at once. It was about acknowledging what was broken and gathering the pieces of myself with gentleness instead of judgment. This scared me. It was about deciding what still belonged to me and what never did.

This is the chapter where my boundaries began to form, not as walls, but as a sort of reclamation. A space where my voice started to return with resolution. I realized this would look like a detachment to others, but it was really a unification of my own wholeness. I had to accept this.

Where my identity began to reassemble itself, not as who I had been, but as who I was now. The little girl wasn't losing her mother, she was growing up and accepting change.

The aftermath wasn't pretty. All I wanted to do was stay in my quiet place and write, to reflect and understand. This is my need right now, my own kind of healing.

This was the moment I stopped pretending everything was fine.
This was the moment I stopped minimizing my own pain.

I began the slow and deliberate work at rebuilding myself, piece by piece, truth by truth.

It was time to keep this little dim flicker alive so it could grow into a bright, big flame and not blow out.

Reflection

The aftermath is where clarity meets reality. It is the moment you see the cost of abandoning yourself, and the possibility of reclaiming what remains. Boundaries form in the rubble. Identity rebuilds itself in the truth before you. This is not the end with the collapse; it is the beginning of becoming whole again.

CHAPTER TEN

THE INTEGRATION

what the body teaches; learning to live differently

For me, integration arrived late, without fanfare.
It didn't feel like a breakthrough or a revelation because I already knew this information. It came in as a steady rearranging, a slow stitching together of everything that broke open. Finding what didn't work anymore and really letting it go.

In the days after, I noticed something subtle happening inside me. My body, which had been screaming for months, began to feel pain. My muscles began to feel like the Tin Man in the Wizard of Oz. The collapse forced me into something I could no longer outrun, and now my body was responding to that.

It was teaching me how to readapt my good habits again. I was a walker. I walked 45 mins to an hour daily. But the last year, I had stopped in order to be there for my mom and support the needs of my sister. I lost the one thing that kept my body healthy; that decision was revealing how big of a mistake that was.

My first lesson was to realign myself with that one thing. It was a lesson in slowness, the slowness of intention. The kind where you pause before saying yes, where you check in with your body before you override it.

For the first time in years, I asked myself simple questions:
What do I need? Is this mine to carry?

Questions I had forgotten to ask.

The second lesson was listening.
Not to the noise around me but to the signals within me.
The tightness in my chest, the pressure in my ears.
The heaviness in my limbs, the burning in my stomach when something wasn't right.

These sensations weren't inconveniences but more information about what didn't work and was harmful to my well being.

My body had been speaking all along. I had simply forgotten how to hear it.

The third lesson was compassion; not for others, but for myself.
This was the hardest one. Caregivers are fluent in compassion for everyone else, but when it comes to ourselves, we ration it like it's scarce.
Integration meant learning to offer myself the same tenderness I had given so freely to others.

It meant acknowledging that I was tired, that I was hurting and that I had limits.
I deserved care, too. I once felt lovable. I needed to know that part of life again. I needed to be loved too.

Integration wasn't a single moment but a series of small choices like choosing rest over guilt, truth in the moment over performance, presence over autopilot. It was learning to inhabit my own life again, not as a role, but as a person.

And slowly, almost imperceptibly, I began to feel something I hadn't felt in a long time: Alignment.

My body and my mind were no longer separated from each other.
My heart and my instincts no longer silenced or suffocated.
My truth and my actions were beginning to match each other. And this was okay.

This was the integration by coherence. A returning to myself, piece by piece, breath by breath.

The collapse was a forced stop. The integration was teaching me how to stay open without falling apart.

Reflection

Integration is the quiet work of becoming whole again. It is the moment you begin listening to your body not as an obstacle, but as a guide. It is the slow, steady alignment of truth, boundaries, and self-compassion. This is where healing becomes a way of living, not a moment of crisis.

CHAPTER ELEVEN

THE OFFERING

giving from fullness, not collapse

Getting to the exhale is what comes next. The moment in healing when the energy that once went into surviving begins to shift towards living in a resolute way. The idea of self-erasing becomes cringey. The thought of over-functioning and over-giving are understood as sacrifice. This is the exhale. It is the moment of pure letting go. And with that comes the ability to give again from joy.

The offering didn't arrive as a decision. It arrived as must. I had no other choice but to listen. It put me in a place that had once held numbness and pressure and ache to offer it defrosting. It was the sense that what I had lived through wasn't meant to stay locked inside me not as a burden, but as learning. A passage that could be shared without costing me safety.

For the first time in a long time, I felt like I had something to give that didn't drain me. Though pangs of electrifying fear would sharply spark in my chest at the thought of sharing my experience with the world. It wasn't advice, instruction or a list of steps or strategies.

It was presence. It was the simple, human offering of saying, *I've been there. I know what it feels like. You're not alone.*

Caregivers are conditioned to give from depletion, to pour from an empty cup, to stretch themselves thin in the name of love or duty. But this offering was different. It came from a place of truce. It was my surrender. I was ready to accept the change ahead knowing everything was not fixed. People were going to be uncomfortable because I surrendered. And caregiving for me was going to have a different shape now. The shape of it was unknown but I made a commitment to still love with all my heart and allow reason to keep the boundary strong.

I realized that the most powerful offering we can give is our light and to always ask with an open heart. Even if it comes unexpectedly or unpolished. I was going to offer love again with a new foundation. It was going to include my own needs too. The real ones. In recap, I vowed to remember:

- The collapse from exhaustion was real.
- When you reach the point of numbness, it is a sign, not a death sentence.
- The body speaks long before the mind is ready to listen.
- Choosing yourself is not selfish but necessary.
- The truth that healing is not linear, but it is possible.
- The truth that this will take a commitment and that it will be a way of life.

I witnessed the teachings in my Book I, right when I finished it and was ready to publish. I was my own observer that what I wrote was factual. These things happen. I was reminded. I want to share that life is synchronistic, and not a preaching. This is real. It's about extending a hand from a place of grounding, not martyrdom.

It's the moment where my story becomes a lantern to light the path just enough for someone else to see their own feet on the ground too.

The offering is simple:
I made it through. You can, too. And you don't have to disappear to do it.

I will admit, this is bittersweet. There is a part of me that knows some might not choose the light, the place of grounding. Knowing this is painful and won't ever go away.

Reflection

The offering is what emerges when healing becomes spacious. It is the moment you can share your truth without losing yourself in the process. It is giving from fullness, not collapse, extending presence instead of sacrifice. Your lived experience becomes a light, not a weight.

CHAPTER TWELVE

THE PATH FORWARD

rebirth, living from truth, not survival

After you experience a collapse and the rebuilding begins, you realize you're no longer within the ruins. You're standing at the edge of them. You can see the mess, all the rubble, and you are at the beginning of the cleanup, shaped by everything you've learned, everything you've survived and reclaimed.

This juncture is important. It is your path forward where you can't really announce: "Here I am." This moment doesn't arrive with certainty, confidence or a five-step plan. It arrives by force, your own bodily force. And for me, was unmistakable.

It showed me the breath that was tight or rushed or stolen between responsibilities.
A breath that felt like it belonged to me but vanished. And how brain cells dye from having missed it.

This arrival doesn't overhaul your life. You don't suddenly become the version of yourself you abandoned years ago. There is definitely a grieving in that. It feels like loss. And it can be harsh. But in taking small steps, you accept where you are; which has changed. A lot. And that is ok. You have to meet yourself here.

This is when I took a small step. It felt almost insignificant until I realized it's the first step I had taken for myself in a really long time.

The forward path isn't about becoming someone new. I understood I couldn't push change that drastically. There wasn't the capacity for that from where I stood. My vantage point wasn't that wide. I had to make the wise decision that this change was going to be incremental.

I accepted this as ok. And knew returning to who I had always been beneath the exhaustion, beneath the roles, beneath the expectations that shaped me into someone I no longer recognized was going to be a long process. So, I adjusted my expectation of outward proof and worked on the internal while tending to the outward.

It decided to choose differently and listen differently.

It was about honouring the signals my body had been sending long before the collapse and trusting the truth that had risen up. I mean, when did I stop listening? I had always listened.

The path forward didn't feel like confidence but felt like an alignment and reorganization. I knew confidence would develop from the alignment in time.

- ✓ It felt like waking up and asking, "*What do I feel and need today?*"
- ✓ It felt like saying no without apology, though I knew apologies would be spoken from me more than occasionally. This was going to be the toughest change.
- ✓ It felt like resting without guilt. Again, probably not always.
- ✓ It felt like speaking without shrinking. This one, I think I was getting better at.
- ✓ It felt like living without disappearing. Well, again like the apology, this would take a lot more effort.

But nonetheless, slowly, step by step, I began to realize something I had forgotten:

Here I was. Alive and capable of self-governance.

I understood I could stop the loop though the path forward may not always be linear. It would bend, wind and pause. It would also circle back. It asks for patience, presence and honesty.

And the strongest reminder for me was and is that the path is mine. I can try my best to shape it without obligation that requires so much sacrifice I lose myself. It doesn't have to always be shaped by crisis, but when it is, I can slow it down and minimize it. And if there is a collapse, I can heal. I have to give it time.

This life is mine. And as I walk it, slowly, intentionally, with my body as my compass and my heart as my guide; I carry one truth with me: I can choose to be the light.

This is the reminder where the path forward stops looping.
It doesn't have to be perfect, but I want for it to be real. I need for it to be authentic and transparent. Hopeful and God driven.

And finally, finally, be mine.

Reflection

The forward path is not a return to who you were because that part of you is gone. It is about starting from where you are. It is the quiet, steady movement toward a life shaped by truth instead of survival. It is the moment you choose to live from alignment, not obligation. This is rebirth: deeply, unmistakably real.

PART III

LETTING GO

INTRODUCTION

The Courage to Release

There is a point in every story when holding on becomes heavier than the fear of what might happen if you finally let go. Part III begins at this threshold.

I find this the most difficult of moments, the one that sits heaviest on my heart even as I try to move through it. I keep reminding myself that letting go is not an act of abandonment. It is an act of truth. It is the moment you stop negotiating with a past that cannot change and stop sacrificing your life to patterns that were built around other people's needs, wounds, and limits. It is the quiet decision to stop carrying the responsibility, the emotional labour, the guilt, the hope that if you just tried harder, the story would turn out differently.

This section is about release and moving forward. It is about loosening the grip that trauma-trained loyalty has had on your body, your choices, and your sense of self. And it is about recognizing that you can love people and still step back. You can care and still choose distance. You can grieve and still move forward.

Letting go is not the end of the relationship with your past. It is the end of your obligation to keep reliving it.

Here is where you begin to reclaim the space that was always meant for you - the space where your voice returns, your boundaries hold, and your life starts to belong to you again. It is the place I find myself in as well, walking this part of the path alongside you.

Part III - Letting Go

When time pushes onward, there is no stopping it. You cannot slow the ticking or the changes that come with aging. There is never a perfect ending. Time creeps up quickly, often unexpectedly, truly unpredictably. Not wanting to let go can turn into holding on too tightly, and right now, I can feel myself doing exactly that.

I am trying hard to remind myself that letting go is not forgetting. I can feel a great change rising ahead of me - one I cannot stop. My hope is that I will find my footing, even if the pain feels sharp and familiar. I can feel myself fading at the edges, the way I do when my heart breaks in the same places. Letting go doesn't erase the past, nor can I pretend it didn't shape me. But I am afraid that if I loosen my grip, the memories will slip away. Like a crack in the earth that you suddenly, shockingly fall into.

My history has meaning; it is woven into my fabric, my core, the deepest parts of who I am. For so long, it has been a defining part of me. Family has been my anchor, my compass and origin. Letting go feels like more than closing a chapter. It feels like reaching the final sequel of a trilogy, and something about that finality terrifies me. I am not fully ready to do this. But then, we never truly are.

My family, with all its vivid memories and complicated emotions, has shaped me in ways I could never deny. Without that history, I would feel unanchored, unrecognizable to myself. Family has always been central to my identity, and honouring that truth matters. But there have been moments when turning toward a new path meant turning slightly away from them, and in those moments, I believed I was betraying them. That belief has weighed heavily on my heart.

I am slowly learning that letting go does not mean betrayal. It means releasing the belief that I must stay defined by what came before. If I honour them in the process - if I hold them dear and declare my love - then I am not betraying anyone by stepping forward, even if my path leads me away for a while or for an indefinite time.

Letting go is the act of releasing someone, something, or some moment back to God - back to its own path and destiny. It is a quiet surrender. For a long time, I believed that love meant carrying everything: the noise, the fear, the tension, the unspoken expectations, the emotional weight of people I adored. I believed loyalty meant doing more. I believed being a good daughter meant being everything.

But the truth is simpler, and yet harder, than that.

I can love my family and still let go of the roles I carried for them. I can honour where I come from without returning to who I had to be. I can remember the child and the woman I was, and grieve what she could not become under the weight of expectations and obligations that were never meant for her.

This is the hardest part: forgiving myself for the changes I didn't see coming, the ones time no longer allows me to return to. Accepting that some goals, some versions of life I once imagined, have passed their window. Time moved while I was busy surviving what was asked of me.

Letting go comes in moments - small, quiet choices like choosing truth over obligation. It is the moment I ask God to meet me where I cannot go alone, and trust that He will appear.

It is the release - the part of the story where I finally walk forward with my own life in my hands again. It is a place I have known before, long ago, before exhaustion settled in and I forgot to wake up inside my own life.

I used to think healing meant going back - staying still, holding onto memories because they felt significant and defining. But sometimes holding on too tightly becomes its own kind of suppression. Memories matter. They shape us, teach us, anchor us. They should never be dismissed or buried. They should be honoured, not cut out or erased to fit a narrative we tell ourselves in order to survive what we've hidden away.

The real question is how to honour them without letting them hold you in place. Letting go is not letting go of the memories. It is releasing the belief that you must live inside them, or allow them to shape a story about you that doesn't include your truth. Letting go means stepping out of that reality. I don't want to place myself in a space where I'm already seen through a lens that isn't true to who I am. As you evolve, your choices evolve with you.

This is where the path stops looping. This is where survival loosens its hold and life begins to be lived from alignment, not duty.

Letting go is the moment someone chooses their truth without apology. Letting go is also maturity. It signifies standing alone. And that can be frightening for someone who has never truly done it.

I had been used to standing alone. But to truly, truly stand alone, you have to truly, truly let go.

Letting go means self-forgiveness. It means accepting that life is made of choices - some conscious, some inherited, some made from fear, some made in love. We choose from a moment, and then we grow with it. When we finally understand that we still have choice, even when it feels like choices were made for us, something inside us alters. Choice is the first step toward becoming fully autonomous. And isn't that the gift God gave us from birth - free will: the right to choose our path, our truth and our destiny.

Today, something in me separated in the healthiest way. I understood how to support my family without merging with their anxieties. It was a breakthrough I didn't expect. For the first time, I realized I didn't need to build a wall to protect myself or lose myself into erasure. I could stay present. I could stay open. I could choose to engage with them from a place of steadiness instead of survival.

I showed them support. I showed them they weren't alone. But I did it without absorbing their fear. Without carrying their panic in my body. Without losing myself in their storms.

Last night, I prayed to God to help them feel how deeply I love them - not through sacrifice or collapse, but through clarity. I asked Him to guide me toward a compassion that doesn't cost me everything. And today, I felt that prayer answered.

I also know now that I cannot take accountability for anyone else's path. My life lesson is not their life lesson. God has His eyes on all of us. I have to remind myself that before me, there is always God - the One supreme power. And if I trust that purely enough, I will find the light even when darkness beckons. Darkness is inevitable, like death. It comes for us all.

My prayer right now is to remain a constant - a source of light that can help nurture and anchor a soul when it is nearing its crossing. I know I cannot stop God from calling someone home. I can ask for more time, and if it is granted, I am blessed. If it is not, it is out of my hands, and I will grieve.

Letting go is trusting that God sees me. It is making peace with the past. It is understanding that every soul walks their path, lives their story, and will one day join God again.

I know I will grieve. I know there will be moments when time freezes and panic rises inside of me. This is a given. Grief comes in seasons - sometimes one, sometimes many. But eventually, there will be a letting go. A new season will arrive, whether it comes in summer or spring, or in the quiet turning of autumn or the stillness of the winter solstice. One day, I will walk openly again and set the grief aside. I will release the weight of pain and step into a new day.

Time will soften the memory, and when it does, I will know that God is cradling my loved one. I will know they are safe. And one day, I will see them again.

Caregivers face grief often. They stare at death too. And it can be overwhelming. It can also be the reason they try so hard. But I want you to know, it won't stop the turning of time.

My hope is that every caregiver who loves from the deepest part of their soul hears this: you can be a grounding presence for your loved one when time shortens and the window begins to close. Be there not to merge with their fear, but to hold the light in their presence so they can feel protected and know they are not alone. There will be angels and loved ones waiting on the other side to carry your work forward. Trust that God has already prepared His helpers.

And with that, I leave you with the one thought I hope you never forget:

Love. Rest. Be.

Wherever you go, love will follow you like a bright light: above you, below you, beside you - and within you! Never, ever let it go.

CLOSING NOTE

There is no perfect way to end a story that is still unfolding. Healing and life don't pause just because we've reached the final page. What I know now is that collapse is not the end of the story. It is the moment the story becomes open.

If you are reading this and something in these pages' echoes inside you, I hope you know this: sometimes what you cannot do, God does for you. Your body responds to the healing sense we all carry within us - our connection to life's unseen divine force, the one that defines our light. Please don't look away from the flame.

This book is simply a witness - a record of what happens when a caregiver finally turns toward herself and listens. My hope is that somewhere in these pages, you've found a reflection of your own truth, a reminder that your needs matter, and permission to choose yourself again, especially if you had forgotten that was possible.

If anything in this book stays with you, let it be this:

Your life belongs to you. No outside permission required.

Please move toward it.
Please listen to your body with reverence, and honour your limits without apology.
May you return to yourself again and again, especially when life feels unfair.

When the path feels heavy or unclear, remember that you are not walking it alone. There is a whole world of us - caregivers, feelers, survivors, rebuilders - learning how to live from truth instead of survival.

This is the end that becomes a beginning. A new cycle of growth. One that is finally, finally yours.

In love, light, and gratitude.

Always,

Alisa

ACKNOWLEDGEMENTS

To every person who has ever felt alone in their caregiving journey: I am sorry for the moments when caring caused you pain, and for the moments when the hurt pierced deeply. For the times you deserved a warm hug or an angelic reprieve and didn't receive it, I am sorry.

My prayer is that in this moment, you hear the message of love you deserve. It is beckoning you to hold it and never let it go. May you feel it, receive it, and never let it go.

AUTHOR'S NOTE

I am not sure when the idea to carve out this book manifested. I have started other novels and somehow, distracted myself away from continuing them and put them aside. This time, I had had enough of staying in the dark, quietly drowning and not coming up for air. Something shifted. I looked at time, what was in front of me and I couldn't stop the process. During the hardest phase of my life, I found courage. Real courage, the kind you have when you face death and everything unimaginable, right in the face! That kind of courage. The kind of courage that pulls you out even though you haven't found your breath yet. That kind.

Suddenly, it dawned on me. This is insane. I realized how much of a caregiver my role throughout the years was. I gave invisibly. I gave unnoticed, without consideration. I gave through personal sacrifice, and career sacrifice. I gave of my time. It was an undesignated role, but constantly demanded. And in that moment of clarity - in the middle of my own agony - something in me was reborn.

I knew I had to see myself differently. I had to put logic and language to more than three decades of unrecognized and undervalued caregiving. And in doing so, I learned something essential: I was not alone. Caregivers like me were everywhere.

Caregivers who looked strong on the outside were actually falling apart on the inside.
Families who loved each other deeply were being torn apart by the chaos trauma brings.
Homes were filled with tension, confusion, and exhaustion because everyone was overwhelmed. These experiences were mine too. Everything became deeply personal.

I've listened to clients in crisis. I've watched nerves break under pressure.

I've guided people out of attempted suicide. I've helped women find shelter when they were being abused. My clients have been like family to me.

I've seen the way trauma spreads through a household and the way caregiving reshapes a person's identity. I've seen the way exhaustion becomes a way of life.

And, I've seen the way healing begins: slowly and quietly when people finally understand what's happening inside their bodies, their relationships, and their homes.

This book is about compassion, clarity and giving language to what has felt unspeakable.
It's about helping families and individuals pause, take a break and find reprieve.

If you recognize yourself in these pages, I want you to know this:
You deserve support, rest, and healing, please take it!

As you step into whatever comes next with all the uncertainty and all the hidden courage you've built along the way, I want you to hold one truth close:

Celebrate your milestones. You've earned them.

RESOURCES & SUPPORT DIRECTORY

These resources are offered as starting points for caregivers seeking support, connection, or additional education. Every family's needs are different, so explore what feels right for you.

Caring Support Organizations

- Local caregiver support groups
- Community centers offering respite programs
- Online caregiver communities and forums
- Veteran family support networks
- Dementia-specific caregiver groups

Mental Health & Emotional Support

- Trauma-informed therapists
- Family counseling services
- Crisis support lines
- 9-8-8 Suicide Crisis Helpline (Canada, call or text)
- Peer-led support circles
- Mindfulness and grounding apps

Dementia & Memory Care Resources

- Alzheimer's and dementia associations
- Alzheimer Society of Canada
- Memory clinics
- Adult day programs
- Respite care providers
- Educational workshops for families

PTSD & Trauma Resources

- Veteran support organizations
- Veterans Affairs Canada support services
- Trauma-informed therapy directories
- Peer support groups
- Somatic and nervous-system-based programs

Practical Support for Daily Living

- Meal support programs
- Transportation services
- Home care agencies
- Community volunteers
- Local respite grants or subsidies

Books & Learning Tools

- Trauma-informed care guides
- Nervous system regulation resources
- Caregiver burnout and resilience books
- Dementia communication guides

This directory is not exhaustive; it's a place to begin and you deserve to access it.

CAREGIVER BILL OF RIGHTS

You have the right to take up space in your own life.
You are a human being with needs, limits, and emotions.

You have the right to rest without guilt.
Rest is a necessity, not a reward.

You have the right to ask for help.
Support is your right. So please ask

You have the right to feel your feelings.
Feel. Without Apology

You have the right to step away when you need space.
Take space. Step Away

You have the right to set boundaries.
Set the hard line, anyway

You have the right to protect your own health.
Protect your spirit, body and mind.

You have the right to a life outside of caregiving.
Your identity is bigger than your responsibilities. Hang on to it.

You have the right to be treated with respect.
Expect acknowledgment, appreciation, and dignity.

You have the right to make mistakes.
Your effort is enough.

You have the right to feel proud of yourself.
What you do matters. Be prideful

You have the right to be cared for too.
Expect compassion, support, and kindness!

You have the right ***not to remain*** *silent.*

Anything you say ***will not*** *be held against you in the court of living!*

SUMMARY OF CORE TOOLS

1. The Nervous System Comes First
Before communication, problem-solving, or caregiving decisions, regulation must happen.
A regulated body creates a regulated home.

2. The Window of Tolerance
Everyone has a zone where they can think clearly, communicate, and stay grounded.
Stress pushes people out of this window into fight, flight, or freeze.
The goal is returning to the window together.

3. Stress Spreads Through a Household
Nervous systems co-regulate.
One persons overwhelm can activate everyone else.
Remember, this is physiology.

4. Micro-Regulation Tools
Small, simple tools that calm the body in real time:

- slow exhale
- grounding through the senses
- orienting to the room
- feeling your feet on the floor
- loosening your jaw and shoulders
- taking a brief pause

These tools interrupt escalation and restore clarity.

5. De-Escalation in Real Families
When things get heated:

- lower your voice

- slow your pace
- reduce language
- give space
- avoid explaining or correcting
- return to safety first

Safety before solutions.

6. Communication That Reduces Conflict

Use short, calm, clear phrases:

- "Let's slow down."
- "I'm listening."
- "We're okay."
- "Let's take a moment."

Tone regulates more than words.

7. Repair After Rupture

Conflict is inevitable. Repair is essential. Keep it simple:

- acknowledge the moment
- take responsibility for your part
- validate their experience
- reconnect gently
- make a small plan for next time

Repair rebuilds trust and is worth it.

8. The Caregiver's Nervous System

Your body absorbs the stress of everyone around you.
You need:

- rest
- boundaries

- support
- moments of joy
- time to breathe

Your well-being is not optional.

9. Asking for Help

You are not meant to carry everything alone.
Support is your infrastructure.

10. Micro-Joy and Micro-Futures

Tiny moments of joy and small things to look forward to help rebuild resilience.
Joy is medicine.

11. Building a Future That Feels Possible

Your future doesn't have to be perfect.

But it can be simpler, flexible, and yours.

12. The Core Truth of This Book

You are not alone. Support is here

CAREGIVER CHEAT SHEET

1. When things escalate, slow everything down.
Lower your voice.
Shorten your sentences.
Move more slowly.
Your calm body helps their body calm.

2. Take one grounding breath before responding.
Inhale gently.
Exhale longer than you inhale.
This resets your nervous system.

3. Use simple, steady phrases.

- "We're okay."
- "Let's slow down."
- "I'm here."
- "Let's take a moment."

Tone matters more than words.

4. When in doubt, reduce stimulation.
Turn down lights.
Lower noise.
Create space.
Fewer inputs = fewer triggers.

5. You don't have to fix the moment - just stabilize it.
Safety first.
Solutions later.

6. If you feel overwhelmed, step away briefly.
A regulated caregiver is the most powerful tool in the room.

7. Repair is more important than perfection.
A simple:
"I'm sorry for my tone earlier."
or
"That was a hard moment."
goes a long way.

8. Micro-joy counts.
A warm drink.
A soft blanket.
A quiet minute.
Small joys rebuild resilience.

9. Ask for help sooner than you think you need it.
You were never meant to carry everything alone.

10. Your needs matter too.
Rest is not optional. Boundaries are not selfish. No is a complete sentence

ABOUT THE AUTHOR

Alisa (Virginia) Carraro is a compassionate, empathic wellness coach and digital experience architect who has spent her career supporting individuals navigate the complex intersections in their lives. Her work blends evidence-based research with deep compassionate coaching, making difficult concepts accessible, practical, and emotionally safe.

She is known for creating clear, actionable tools that help stabilize crisis moments, communicate more effectively, and rebuild connection after chaos. Her approach is grounded, sensitive, and rooted in the belief that healing becomes possible when people feel seen, supported, and understood.

Alisa's work extends across digital education, care advocacy, and online support. She specializes in helping individuals make sense of behaviors that feel confusing or overwhelming, offering guidance that is both scientifically informed and deeply personal.

When she's not writing or coaching, Alisa is building scalable systems that make support more accessible to the people who need it most. Her mission is simple: to empower individuals with the knowledge, tools, and compassion they deserve; and to remind them that they are never alone.

THANK YOU FOR READING

Thank you for spending your time, energy, and heart with this book.

My hope is that these pages offer you understanding, validation, and a sense of companionship in the places and stages when you've felt alone. I hope you've found tools that are doable, language that feels grounding, and reminders that lighten the weight you carry.

Most of all, I hope you leave this book knowing that your personal story matters and so does your right to share it.

Thank you for letting me walk beside you. I have always accepted that when a client calls me for a coaching session, it might be enough. They may take flight immediately. So, I urge you now: Take flight, flap your wings when you put this book down. Soar! I will be there, in the background like a wind machine, sending the power your way so you keep flying **"Sky High!"**

STAY CONNECTED

If this book supported you, I invite you to stay connected and explore more tools designed to help anyone in trauma dynamics.

You can find additional resources, articles, and guided support at:
https://CarraroMedia.com

On the website, you'll also find companion apps created to support you in real time:

1.Dementia Care Companion
A gentle, practical tool for families supporting loved ones with dementia.
It offers communication guidance, behavior explanations, and in-the-moment strategies to reduce overwhelm.

2.Guided Support
A trauma-informed resource for grounding, regulation, and emotional stabilization.
It's designed to help you navigate crisis moments, calm your nervous system, and reconnect with yourself.

Continued...

3.Mood Blossom

A personalized companion just for you! To help regulate your mood patterns.

4. 1ST SHIELD™ — Resilience Support for First Responders

The newest pillar of our privacy-first support ecosystem, engineered for the high-stakes realities of First Responders. Built first for the Canadian Frontline with global outreach to come, it is currently in a pilot phase only and not commercially available or distributed to the public.

www.ingramcontent.com/pod-product-compliance
Lightning Source LLC
LaVergne TN
LVHW010716061126
851857LV00014B/1213
* 9 7 8 1 0 6 7 7 9 0 9 0 5 *